HOUSES
of
NOBLE POVERTY

HOUSES of NOBLE POVERTY

A History of the English Almshouse

by

BRIAN HOWSON

*This book has been
sponsored by Mrs Jean Follett Holt
in memory of her late husband
Colonel Frank Reginald Follet Holt T.D.
and is published in conjunction with
The Almshouse Association.*

BELLEVUE BOOKS

First published in 1993
by Bellevue Books in conjunction with
The Almshouse Association.

British Library Cataloguing in Publication Data.

A CIP record of this book is available from the British Library.

ISBN 1 873335 02 4

Typeset by Laws & Stimson Associates, New Malden, Surrey.

Printed by Whitstable Litho Printers Ltd, Whitstable, Kent.

Designed by Bob Hall.

Contents

Foreword

The almshouse movement has a history of over 1,000 years. The first hospices were just that; places for the care of the sick poor. The modern almshouse, on the other hand, is a self-contained small house or flat for the elderly – but still for the poor elderly and often with warden care to provide for minor illness. In just a few, as for example, the Great Hospital in Norwich, full nursing-home care is also available.

Throughout the ages there has been a common theme of care and shelter for the elderly poor, but the way in which it has been provided has varied to accommodate the changing social patterns. In this book Brian Howson places the development of almshouses in the context of the social and economic history of the last 1,000 years and at the same time covers comprehensively the architectural development both in the text and with copious illustrations.

As Treasurer for the past 30 years of The National Association of Almshouses I have naturally spent some time in fund-raising for the Association and the argument I have consistently used, and in which I do firmly believe, has been that almshouses are worthy of support for two quite separate reasons. Most important, of course, is that they enable people to retain the dignity and the stimulus of living in decent independent accommodation in their old age, however small their means, and often with the benefit of nursing care at hand but never obtrusive. The second benefit is the preservation of some of the most attractive features of both our urban and our rural heritage. The purpose for which almshouses are built has dictated a scale in their architecture which is particularly attractive to the eye and peaceful to the spirit.

The National Association of Almshouses is dedicated to the promotion of the best standards of care and to the preservation of wonderful buildings. I therefore welcome this book for the way in which it so comprehensively covers both aspects of the history of almshouses. It has to be the definitive book on the subject, although only for so long. For I am confident that the almshouse movement will continue to adapt and to react to the changing needs of the times and who knows what further changes there may be in the next 100, let alone the next 1,000 years.

Sir David Money-Coutts K.C.V.O.
Coutts and Co., 1993

7

List of Figures

List of Plates

Introduction

The care of the elderly has become big business in recent years, both in the public and private sectors. As improvements in medical science and health care have prolonged life, more and more specialised accommodation has become necessary for the aged. It ranges from one or two bedroom bungalows for those growing old gracefully, to what are known as " frail, elderly nursing homes" for those who although continuing to survive, are in need of almost constant care and attention to provide for their daily needs.

The current preoccupation with geriatric care is by no means new. We have in this country a well-established and well-documented tradition of provision for our old folk, predominantly charitable in origin, and reaching back over a thousand years. The organisations providing this care are known generically as almshouse charities.

This work aims to outline the development of almshouses from their origins as mediaeval hospitals and adjuncts of the monastic system, through the Tudor and Stuart periods when they were provided by both craft guilds and under the wills of country gentlemen, to Georgian and Victorian times when they became more urban in character and philanthropic in sponsorship.

They survive into the present century in substantial if sometimes unrecorded numbers. Over 25,000 strong in small groupings of from four to ten dwellings, they exist in many cases unnoticed in almost every town in the land, still housing the less well-off although thankfully not, as in the past, those in absolute penury.

With such a large number of almshouse groups – over 2,300 recorded as being currently occupied and an unknown number now used for other non-residential purposes – it has obviously not been possible for the author to visit each and every one. It has been necessary therefore to rely to a great extent upon research by others gone before, together with help from those in the present day who have generously given of their time and experience.

Acknowledgement must firstly be made to the three pioneers of almshouse lore; the Victorian architect F.T.Dolman's *Hospitals of the Middle Ages* published in 1858, Miss Rotha Mary Clay's *The Mediaeval Hospitals of England* published in 1909 and Walter H. Godfrey's *The English Almshouse* published in 1955. Their seminal research formed the armature upon which the body of this book is wound. Two other recently published works also stand out as being major contributions to the current body of knowledge; Brian Bailey's *Almshouses*, published in 1988, with its comprehensive list of charities great and small in town and village, and Clive Berridge's *The Almshouses of London*, published in 1987, which covers almshouse charities past and present in the metropolis. Whilst most of the photographs for this volume were taken by the author, he is indebted to Clive Berridge for his permission to reproduce Plates 67 and 68 from his own work.

Many individuals have been of assistance during the several years of research which led to the publication of this volume and it would be difficult if not impossible to acknowledge each and every one's contribution. However one individual and one organisation must be singled out for special mention. David Scott and his staff at the Almshouse Association's headquarters at Wokingham have given unstinting help and support. Their detailed knowledge of and care for all the almshouses of the British Isles, together with their comprehensive database of charities registered with the Association, have been invaluable. David's own extensive personal knowledge, not only of buildings but also of personalities, almsfolk as well as trustees, reminds the author that this study deals only with the larger well-known and well-documented institutions.

Numerous small local charities remain scattered throughout the land whose trustees, often in the prime of life themselves, give freely of their time and resources, keeping alive the traditions of parochial service which has been fostered during a thousand years of history. It is to these largely unsung and unrewarded philanthropists that this volume is dedicated.

Brian Howson
Brighouse, 1993

Chronology

816   Synod of Aix, France.

986   Hospital of St. Peter, York, North Yorkshire (later refounded in 1135 by King Stephen as St. Leonard's Hospital).

1089   Harbledown Hospital, Canterbury, Kent by Archbishop Lanfranc.

1123   St. Bartholomew's Hospital, London by Raher.

1136   Hospital of St. Cross, Winchester, Hampshire by Henry de Bois.

1200   St. John's Hospital, Northampton, Northants by William Sancte Clere.

1249   The Great Hospital, Norwich, Norfolk by Walter de Suffield.

1331   Newarke Hospital, Leicester, Leicestershire by Henry Earl of Lancaster.

1437   Hospital of SS. John the Baptist and Evangelist, Sherborne, Dorset.

1437   Ewelme Hospital, Oxfordshire by William de la Pole.

1485   William Browne's Hospital, Stamford, Lincolnshire.

1517   Hospital of the Savoy, London by King Henry VII.

1539   Dissolution of the monasteries.

1571   Lord Leycester's Hospital, Warwick, Warwickshire (conversion from Guildhall).

1592   Forde's Hospital, Coventry, West Midlands.

1596   Holy Trinity Hospital, Croydon, London, by Archbishop Whitgift.

1611   The Charterhouse, London (Converted to almshouses from Carthusian monastery by Thomas Sutton).

1639   Almshouses at Moretonhampstead, Devon.

1670   Les Invalides, Paris, France.

1684   Kilmainham Hospital, Dublin, Ireland.

1686   The Royal Hospital, Chelsea, London.

1694   The Royal Naval Hospital, Greenwich, London.

1695   Morden College, Blackheath, London.

1695   Trinity Almshouses, Mile End Road, London.

1707   Twitty's Almshouses, Abingdon, Oxon.

1733   Sarah, Duchess of Marlborough's Almshouses, St. Albans, Hertfordshire.

1826 Licensed Victuallers' Homes, Peckham, London.

1836 Tyne Master Mariners' Asylum, Tynemouth, Tyne and Wear.

1840 Dr. Caleb Crowther's Almshouses, Wakefield, West Yorkshire.

1844 Aberford Almshouses, Aberford Nr. Leeds, West Yorkshire.

1856 Bradford Tradesmen's Homes, Bradford, West Yorkshire.

1881 United Westminster Almshouses, Westminster, London.

1897 Diamond Jubilee Almshouses, Whippingham, Isle of Wight.

1898 Durham Aged Mineworkers' Homes, County Durham.

1900 Linen and Woollen Drapers' Homes, Mill Hill, London.

1919 North-east Railway Cottage Homes, Darlington, Co. Durham.

1921 Whiteley Village, Surrey.

1946 The Almshouse Association.

1986 Service in Westminster Abbey to commemorate 1000 years of almshouses.

Chapter 1

Monastic Beginnings

Bedehouse, hospital, spital, maison dieu, domus dei, lazer-house, mallardy, almshouse – such were the various names given to all those institutions which have come down to us under the generic name almshouse.

To most people the English almshouse is merely a picturesque reminder of a bygone age, an anachronism which seems to have very little place in the Welfare State of twentieth century Britain. It comes as something of a surprise therefore, to learn that there are some two thousand separate groups in existence throughout the country, most of them of ancient origin, still providing much needed accommodation for upwards of twenty-thousand elderly people. Moreover, they are still being built and rebuilt today in modest numbers, and with some modifications are all administered in much the same way as they were in times gone by. Equally surprising is just how old the almshouse tradition is, and how closely it is interwoven with other strands of our daily life.

As with many of our social institutions in Britain, almshouses had their origins in early mediaeval times, as a result directly or indirectly of the monastic revolution which smouldered away during the Anglo-Saxon centuries following the introduction of Christianity by Augustine and Patrick, and which burst into life after the Norman Conquest of 1066. In the wake of this maelstrom the new Norman masters carved up the country-side between them and in doing so made generous provision for the religious who accompanied them, granting sites for their new monasteries and endowing them with large tracts of land to provide them with an income.

Since the Synod of Aix in 816 A.D., one of the tenets – indeed the cornerstone of the new monasticism – was the distribution of alms, the very basis of the seven Corporal Works of Mercy. Every religious house was under an obligation to distribute alms, which usually consisted of food, clothing, medicine and occasionally money, but which could also take the form of board and lodging and even education. The official charged with the duty of collecting and distributing alms was the almoner whose role until recently was echoed in the post of almoner in the modern hospital, in charge of patients' welfare.

During the later mediaeval period, the education function was hived off. Although universities throughout Europe developed without the direct involvement of the monasteries, because of their need to acquire learning to fulfil their spiritual obligations in quire, the greater houses felt it necessary to become involved, and in 1283 the Abbot of Gloucester founded a college in Oxford for the use of monks; Durham followed in 1290 on the site now occupied by Trinity. Ely followed suit, founding a college, now Trinity Hall in Cambridge in 1340, and Crowland a hostel in 1428, which subsequently became Buckingham College. At the lower end of the scale, some houses in the towns provided education for poor children, usually through the almonry and its schools where some children were boarded. Such was Durham where the "children of the almonry" were fed, clothed and educated at the abbey's expense. Many nunneries also took in girl boarders to supplement their income and it was from these beginnings that the custom of convent education grew.

At first the almoner distributed his alms at the gate of the convent; the almoner's window can still be seen at Dorchester and Evesham. Gradually the practice grew of providing board and lodging for travellers within the curia or outer court of the monastery itself, in the guest house for the more well-to-do, and in a separate building, the hospitum for the ordinary traveller.

Monks had always made provision for their own sick, aged and infirm brothers in the farmery (from which the name infirmary is derived), usually on the quiet side of the precinct away from the hustle and bustle of the outer court. They were provided with a hall with bed spaces along the outside walls, a special kitchen where nourishing meals could be provided, and a chapel, usually at the end of the hall where the brothers could see the altar from their beds.

One of the best documented farmery buildings is that attached to Fountains Abbey near Ripon in North Yorkshire, undoubtedly the most perfectly preserved Cistercian house in the whole of the country. Although the walls of the farmery and its associated buildings have long since disappeared, enough remains to conjecture how the building looked in its heyday at the beginning of the thirteenth century. Indeed, the Department of the Environment, the custodians of the buildings have gone so far as to construct a model of the whole monastery at the scale of an eighth of an inch to one foot with the details of the missing superstructure being derived from the style of the existing buildings on site, together with examples of Cistercian architecture elsewhere.

Figure 1 shows the plan form of the farmery as it existed about 1240. The great hall measuring some 180 feet by 78 feet was one of the largest in mediaeval Britain and originally had bed spaces round the walls, with fireplaces in the northern and southern gables. To the east lay chambers thought to have been occupied by retired abbots, the chapel and kitchen of the latter separated from the hall by passages and yards as a precaution against fire. Plate 1 shows a view of the model from the south-east.

During the twelfth and thirteenth centuries, hospitals within the walls of the monastery took on the form of the farmery with hall and chapel. As well as for travellers they began to cater for the poor, aged and infirm laymen and women, providing alms on site as board and lodging. The day-to-day caring for the inmates was carried out by brothers (or sisters in the case of nunneries) and lay assistants, but gradually the practice of ministering to lay people within the monastery proper ceased and separate hospitals were built well away from the establishment, usually in a nearby town but often many miles away.

To begin with, these separate hospitals were also administered by the religious, who were usually tonsured as were their brethren in the closed community. They were assisted by lay brothers, all living under a modified Rule, usually that of St. Benedict. Like the greater houses, they were endowed with their own lands and properties and other investments to provide an income to finance the good works. Very few of these early hospitals have survived as solely medical establishments, although one stands out particularly. This is St. Bartholomew's Hospital, Smithfield, affectionately known as "Bart's" which was founded as a mediaeval hospital in 1123 by a monk named Rahere, and has continued to provide medical care on the same site for the past eight hundred years.

From the eleventh to the fourteenth centuries, the need for refuge and care was increased substantially by the incidence of leprosy which spread like the plague throughout the whole of Western Europe. .

Leprosy is generally considered to have been introduced by Crusaders returning from the Holy Land. Indeed, as Voltaire phlegmatically declared: "all that we gained in the end by engaging in the Crusades was leprosy; and of all that we had taken, that was the only thing that remained with us". This was not entirely true, for lepers were known to have existed in England in Saxon times, and at least two lazer-houses, as leper hospitals were known, had been established within twenty years of the Conquest, well before the first Crusade was mounted. There is no doubt that the disease was at its most virulent during the early mediaeval centuries, gradually dying out by the late 1400s.

While it lasted, the poor afflicted were ostracised and driven from the urban areas and forced to live out their lives in abject poverty and loneliness. Indeed, legislation was introduced locally, nationally and from Rome itself, which enforced the removal of lepers from contact with their more fortunate brethren. The writ *de leprose amorendo* of 1150 authorised the expulsion of lepers on account of "manifest peril by contagion" and the Papal Canon of 1179 declared emphatically that lepers could not dwell with healthy men.

Looking back, it is clear that the word leprosy covered a whole range of diseases of a malforming nature. Scrofula, tuberculosis, erysipelas,

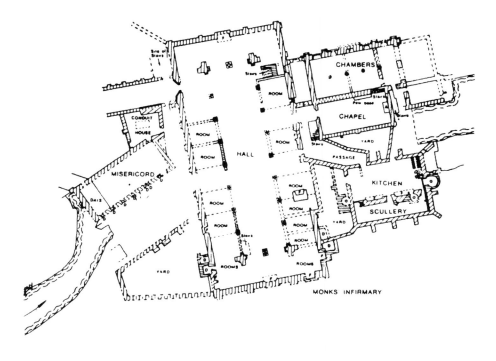

Fig 1. Plan of Farmery, Fountains Abbey, North Yorkshire.

19

elephantiasis and diseases contracted by persons "as a baneful result of a life stained by sin", were all lumped together under the blanket term leprosy.

A lazer was one "full of sores"; any person suffering from a disfiguring skin eruption was considered to be infected. Paradoxically, it was not the fear of infection itself which engendered the expulsion of lepers, but revulsion at the sight of such "hideous and noisome objects". The poor wretch, clad in a sombre cloak and cowl hiding his grey and wasted body, limbs maimed and stunted, hobbled or crawled along, his features ulcerated and sunken, his eyes unsightly and unseeing, his gravelly voice entreating help, extending "supplicating lazer arms with clapper and alms dish".

The two earliest lazer-houses founded, as mentioned before, prior to 1100, were Harbledown near Canterbury and Rochester. Harbledown was founded by Abbot Lanfranc (1005-89), William the Conqueror's first Archbishop of Canterbury, a mile or so outside the city and dedicated to St. Leonard; Rochester was founded by Bishop Gundolph and dedicated to St. Bartholomew. Of the two, only Rochester's hospital building remains, much enlarged and changed almost beyond recognition (see Figure 2), standing in Chatham High Street and now used as a church. Harbledown's church remains, now surrounded by more modern accommodation.

Although upwards of two hundred and fifty lazer-houses were founded during the early mediaeval period, many have long since disappeared as the need for them has thankfully evaporated. But one or two remain and are to this day the very backbone of the modern almshouse movement. Two of the oldest illustrate the vicissitudes through which these old institutions have gone during the eight centuries or so since their foundation.

The first, Sherburn Hospital, situated two miles or so to the south of Durham City, was founded in 1181 by Bishop Hugh de Puiset as a house for sixty-five lepers in five convents of thirteen. Each convent was ministered to by a chaplain, the whole hospital being controlled by a master and endowed with land and property.

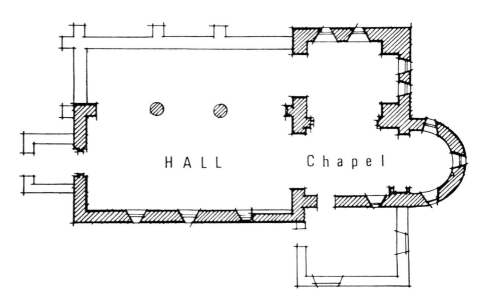

Fig 2. Plan of Rochester Hospital, Chatham, Kent.

Despite being badly damaged during the Battle of Neville's Cross in 1346, the year of Crécy, it survived as a lazer-house until 1434, when it was appropriated for other uses and the places of the sixty-five lepers were taken by thirteen poor men unable to support themselves by their own means. Places for two lepers were kept "if they can be found in those parts", but in effect the hospital was transformed into an almshouse, where: "in that haunt of ancient peace many are now sheltered in time of age and sickness".

Buildings were variously erected and demolished during its eight hundred year history. Figure 3 shows a drawing of the hospital as it existed in 1781; the church, gateway and the range nearest to the lower margin still remain. In Victorian times a large hospital block was erected to the west of the church which was used for medical purposes until the advent of the National Health Service after the Second World War. Now over one hundred and fifty men and women are housed in a wide variety of accommodation; in the old mediaeval range, in the Victorian hospital block, in the Elizabethan gatehouse and in other purpose-built flats in the grounds. The master and his wife, the Head of Care, reside in half of the Georgian master's house to the east of the church, with the other half together with extensions, housing five retired clergymen and their wives. Figure 4 shows a current plan of the hospital, whilst Plate 2 shows Sherburn Hospital as it is today looking into the grounds through the gateway.

The second lazer-house, St. Mary Magdalene at Ripon, was founded a few years earlier than Sherburn in 1139 by the Abbot of Ripon, Archbishop Thurston. It was originally a shelter for wayfaring lepers, where they could count on food and shelter and had its own chapel where the lepers could worship in isolation. By 1317 lepers ceased to frequent the hospital "because applicants went away empty-handed", and a later inquiry showed that the lazer-house had fallen down. It did, however,

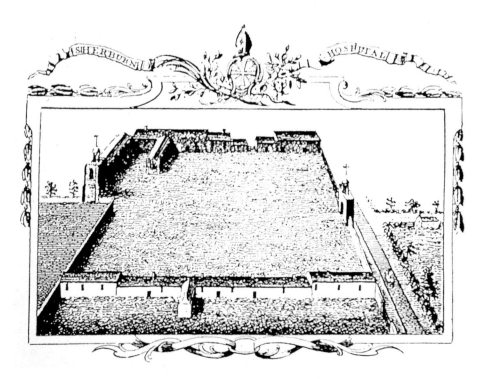

Fig 3. Sherburn Hospital, Durham, County Durham, 1781.

continue as a hospital for the elderly and infirm, and today has two groups of almshouses, one on either side of Stonebridgegate, together with two chapels, one a Victorian building of no particular interest, and the other the original leper chapel very much as it was when built in the twelfth century.

As with Sherburn, the Mary Magdalene trustees, drawn from the townspeople of Ripon with the Dean of Ripon Cathedral – the erstwhile abbot – as their chairman, are still anxious to provide for the parishioners of the town, and have plans to build further cottages on land they own nearby. Plate 3 shows the leper chapel as it exists today.

There are many relics of these early hospitals lurking away unnoticed by modern society. In the centre of bustling Gateshead town centre St. Edmund's parish church was originally the chapel of St. Edmund's Hospital founded in 1247 and restored in Victorian times (Plate 4). Domus Dei, Portsmouth, built in 1229 is now part of the garrison church and St. John's, Northampton of 1140 is now used as a Roman Catholic church. We shall return to some of these important buildings later.

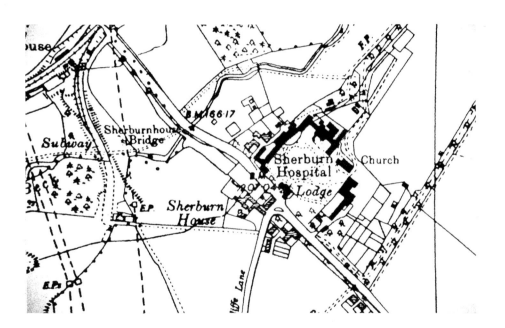

Fig 4. Plan of Sherburn Hospital, Durham, County Durham, today.

Plate 1. Model of Farmery, Fountains Abbey, North Yorkshire.

Plate 2. Sherburn Hospital, Durham, County Durham.

Plate 3. Chapel, Hospital of St. Mary Magdalene, Ripon, North Yorkshire.

Plate 4. St. Edmund's Hospital Chapel, Gateshead, Tyne and Wear.

24

Chapter 2

Founders and Benefactors

The monastic orders were by no means the only providers of hospitals.

In mediaeval Europe, travel between towns was an inconvenient and sometimes hazardous business, more so between different countries. Because of the lack of decent roads, only short distances could be covered each day either on foot or, if one were fortunate, by coach or on horseback. As interchange between towns and cities increased for administrative or trade reasons, there developed an increasing need for frequent stopping places along the principal routes and with the absence of what we now know as hotels or inns, hostels and hospitals were established for travellers, situated close to the gateways of important towns.

Moreover, the early mediaeval period was above all a time of pilgrimage, with sufferers from various diseases making long and difficult journeys to the principal shrines of Europe in the hope that some miracle would transform their lives. These hopeful wayfarers constituted an increasingly important element in the travelling public and were the principal users of hospital accommodation in certain towns. At the important shrine of Bury St. Edmunds, the remains of five hospitals can still be seen: St. Saviour outside the North Gate, St. John the Evangelist outside the South Gate, St. Stephen and St. Nicholas outside the East Gate and St. Peter outside the Risby Gate.

Many other regional centres had similar numbers of hospitals. Figure 5 shows the situation of mediaeval hospitals within the town of Beverley, an important centre of the wool trade in East Yorkshire. Hospitals for travellers, pilgrims and lepers as well as for the aged and infirm were situated there, together with two friaries.

Remains of the original hospitals have long since disappeared, although Plate 5 does give an indication of how the Hospital of St. Mary the Blessed Virgin outside the North Gate appeared. Many of the hospitals still live on though in a slightly different guise, having been transformed into almshouses for the elderly and infirm in the post-Reformation period. The bedehouses in Liargate, which are thought to have been built on the site of the early mediaeval hospital dedicated to St. Giles, show their hospital origins by their name since a bedesman was the occupier of a hospital who, in return for his keep, said daily prayers for the founder or benefactor.

These non-monastic hospitals were founded and endowed by a broad cross-section of benefactors. Top of the list was the clergy – mainly bishops and archbishops – who saw it as part of their spiritual duty to set an example in the provision of charitable works. Most cathedral towns had several hospitals and almshouses. Ripon, though only a small market town had three, all of which survive to this day as almshouses. St. Mary Magdalene, the lazer-house in Stonebridgegate has already been referred to. The others, dedicated to St. John the Evangelist and St. Anne, lie within walking distance of the cathedral. Both now provide modern accommodation, although St. Anne's in High St. Agnesgate still retains the ruins of the original twelfth century chapel in the grounds of the Victorian cottages.

Worcester was another cathedral city with hospitals founded and endowed by bishops, although their independence was long disputed and resented by the priory. Of the three mediaeval hospitals which existed prior to the Reformation, only the one founded by and later dedicated to St. Wulston, the last Saxon Bishop in England, has a history which has been handed down to the present day. The date of the foundation is uncertain, although it must have been prior to 1095, the date of Wulston's death. It was certainly known as St. Wulston's Hospital a few years after 1203 when the bishop was canonised.

The hospital was established as an almshouse for the aged, situated outside the Sidbury (i.e. South) gate, just one hundred yards or so from the cathedral. Wulston endowed the hospital with lands for its upkeep and in subsequent years gifts of land and tithes of property were donated in Worcester itself and elsewhere in Worcestershire and the surrounding counties, such as the following which were included in an inventory confirmed by King Henry III (1207-72) at Tewkesbury in 1232:

"...of the gift of Osbert de Abbetot all the land with out the gate of Suthbiri (Sidbury) which is held of Hugh de Say. Of the gift of Richard de

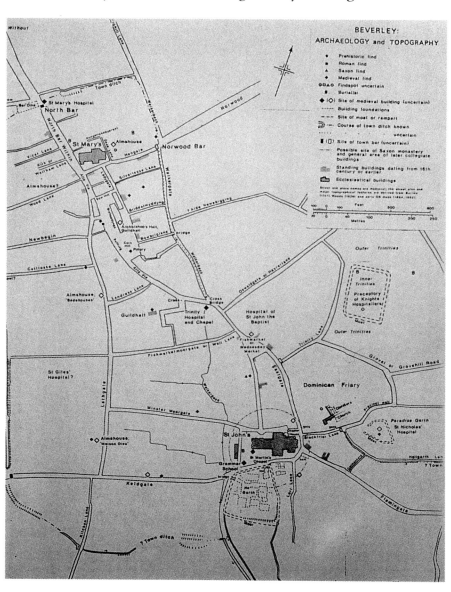

Fig 5. Map of mediaeval Beverley, North Yorkshire.

Acre 2 shillings of rent in Kideminster. Of the gift of William Crasus the first-born a burgage in his borough of Sobbyry (Sidbury). Of the gift of Tomo the hunter 4 shillings of rent in Croule....."

In 1487 the income of the hospital from all sources was £159.5s.2d, the highest that it ever attained; at its suppression in 1540, it was valued at £79.12s.6d.

In its early days the hospital was administered by a master (who did not necessarily have to be a priest), assisted by two chaplains and poor brethren, all living under the Rule of St. Augustine. No accurate record of the number of inmates exists although it has been ascertained that in 1294 there were twenty-two feeble residents in the infirmary. In the same year the hospital received a handsome gift of sixty marks and ten pounds sterling from one William de Molendis, a clerk, in return for which he was to have the benefit of Masses and prayers in the chapel, together with the right to nominate three poor chaplains in the infirmary, with beds "in a decent place". This practice of granting board and lodging to poor people in return for an initial cash payment, known as a corrody, was continued in the fourteenth and fifteenth centuries by the Master William Dylew. There is a record that in 1396 Thomas Croke was granted "to the end of his life one chamber built recently near the gate of the hospital" and again in 1403 Nicholas and Sybil Baily were allocated "a good chamber with a fireplace and a privy".

This granting of corrodies was frowned upon as an abuse of the charitable role of the hospital, and in 1441 Bishop Bourchier brought about reforms and drew up new ordinances which specified that in future the master should be a priest in holy orders, that there were to be two chaplains, five poor brethren and two poor sisters only, and that the granting of corrodies was forbidden. The chaplains were each to have an allowance of four marks yearly, a chamber to themselves and three and a half yards of cloth for a gown. The brethren and sisters, who were to join in daily prayer for the souls of their predecessors, founders, patrons and benefactors were allowed seven pence each a week. The affairs of the hospital were to be conducted under seal (see Figure 6) and the renting out of property was not to be undertaken without the consent of the brethren and sisters; in effect, the hospital became a corporate body.

Strangely enough, in 1298 the hospital became known as The Preceptory or Commandery of St. Wulston, in imitation of the military religious orders of the Knights Templar and Hospitallers, but there is as yet no proof of any connection with the Hospitallers either at Worcester or nearby Dinmore. However, it has been known as the Commandery ever since. Along with most monasteries and many hospitals, the Commandery was suppressed by Henry VIII (1491-1547) following his break with the Catholic church, and was purchased by its last master, Richard Morysyne for just £14.3s.5d! He sold the buildings on five years later to a clothier "in consideration of four hundred and four score and eighteen pounds of good and lawful money of England". Quite a profit! Subsequently, it remained in residential use, although during the Civil War (in 1651) it served as the headquarters of Charles II (1630-85) during the Battle of Worcester. It survives today as a tourist centre and museum. Plate 6 shows the building as it exists now.

Fig 6. Seal of St. Wulston's Hospital, Worcester, Hereford and Worcester.

Of the non-clerical founders, by far the most important was royalty itself. One of the earliest recorded foundations was the Hospital of St. Leonard at York which was, incidentally, the largest known hospital in the land, housing at one time over two hundred and twenty inmates who were cared for by a staff of over two dozen. In addition to a housekeeper, the materfamilias, and a master " de farmaria", there were sixteen male and female servants, two or three bakers, brewers, smiths, carters, ferrymen as well as the usual chaplains. The hospital was founded by King Athelstan, a Saxon monarch, although when he founded it in 986 it was dedicated to St. Peter. It fell into disuse after a major fire and was refounded by King Stephen (1105-54) in 1145 and dedicated to St. Leonard.

York was second only in importance to London in mediaeval times, and it can be imagined that the Hospital of St. Leonard was kept busy catering for a wide range of almspeople and travellers having business in York. Very little of the hospital remains other than the ruins of the chapel and its undercroft standing in the grounds of the Yorkshire Museum in Museum Street. Plate 7 shows the interior of the undercroft with its typical Norman vaulting.

King Stephen's wife, Matilda, also founded a famous hospital, St. Catherine-by-the-Tower, London in 1148. It was always under the special patronage of the kings and queens of England. Queen Eleanor, the wife of Richard Coeur de Lion (1157-99) established its independence from the priory at Aldgate in 1261; Queen Philippa endowed it in 1351; Henry VI (1421-71) gave it a new charter in 1442; even Henry VIII founded the Guild of St. Barbara there and spared the hospital from suppression, the fate of all monasteries and most hospitals following his split with Rome in 1539. It survived until the Victorian era when St. Catherine's Dock was built on its site.

Surprisingly enough, King John (1169-1216), generally regarded as a rogue and usurper, is thought to have founded several hospitals, at Lancaster, Newbury and Bristol. He is regarded as a conspicuous patron of lepers. Bale in his play *Kynge John* describes him thus:

"never prynce was there that made to poor peoples use so many masendewes, hospytals and spytle houses, as your grace has done yet sens the worlde began".

Henry VIII provided houses at Woodstock, Dunwich and Ospring, homes for Jews in London and Oxford as well as rebuilding St. John's, Cambridge, St. James', Westminster and St. John's, Oxford. He was especially fond of Gloucester, the place of his coronation, re-establishing and endowing the Hospital of St. Bartholomew there.

We cannot leave royalty without reference to the founders of perhaps the two most famous hospitals in England; that at Chelsea occupied by retired soldiers, and the Royal Hospital at Greenwich, planned originally as a palace but converted before completion into a hospital for aged seamen. Both were built by Stuart monarchs during a period when many charitable institutions were founded. Chelsea, designed wholly by Sir Christopher Wren (1632-1725) was commissioned by Charles II, whereas that at Greenwich, designed only in part by Wren, was founded by his niece Mary, the consort of William of Orange. We shall be returning to both these important almshouses later.

Next to royalty in importance were the landowning gentry and aristocracy who, perhaps above all others, endowed the majority of small country almshouses whose sole purpose was to provide for the aged poor of the parish.

It is easy to forget that in the later feudal and mediaeval period the Lords of the Manor were just that, lords of all their domain, with in most cases power of life and death over the people who resided there. Most of their land and property was vested in the title they bore, handed down from generation to generation, and the villeins, serfs and peasants were treated almost in the same manner as the animals with which they shared an existence.

Later, as first copyhold and then freehold tenures were introduced, the more astute were able to acquire their own land and buildings, but overall the majority of workers lived in rented, generally tied accommodation. Not having the pensions or annuities which are the norm today, poor people at the end of their working lives were forced to rely either on their children to support them or, failing that, whatever charity was available. In Victorian times they had the doubtful benefit of relying on the Poor Law Institute or workhouse.

Out of compassion for the plight of such aged poor or, more likely, in order to provide for their own retired retainers, the gentry built small groups of cottages, or sometimes merely one-room dwellings under the supervision of the estate overseer, or the parish priest.

A classic, if somewhat unusual, example of such a group of dwellings is that known as Beamsley Hospital near Skipton in North Yorkshire, although the building has recently ceased to be occupied as an almshouse. It was begun in 1593 by the Countess of Cumberland and completed in 1650 by her daughter Ann Clifford, the Countess of Pembroke who was at the time the occupier of nearby Skipton Castle. The accommodation comprised seven one-room dwellings clustered round a minute chapel. What was most unusual though was the building's shape; it was circular like the churches of the two military monastic orders, the Knights Templar and Knights Hospitaller, although there is no evidence to suggest any connection with either. Figure 7 shows a plan of the hospital before its conversion into a private house and Plate 8 as it appears today.

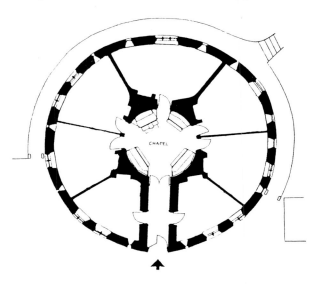

Fig 7. Plan of Beamsley Hospital, Craven, North Yorkshire.

29

An earlier example of a foundation by a member of the aristocracy is that originally known as Newarke Hospital in Leicester. This hospital with the distinction of having the longest hall in the country – over two hundred feet in length – was founded by Henry Earl of Leicester in 1351, to house fifty poor men, with accommodation for master, chaplain and staff. The hospital was later enlarged by his son Henry, Duke of Leicester, who added a collegiate church with a dean and twelve canons. When enlarged, the whole establishment had, besides the canons, twelve vicars, three clerks, six choristers and ten nurses who cared for one hundred in-pensioners, fifty men and fifty women. Originally dedicated to the Annunciation of the Virgin Mary, it was again reconstituted in the seventeenth century and renamed Trinity Hospital. Figure 8 shows a plan of the original hospital.

In order of importance, after the aristocracy came the foundations of the ordinary gentry, petty knights and baronets, merchants, philanthropists, aldermen and burgesses, and particularly Lord Mayors of the City of London.

A famous example of the latter is that founded by Sir William Turner, the Lord Mayor of London who supervised the rebuilding of the capital after the Great Fire of 1666, at the place of his birth, Kirkleatham, near Redcar in Cleveland. It is thought that Wren had a hand in the design since he and Sir William were friends.

Turner's Hospital was originally founded in 1676, although it was completely remodelled by Sir William's great-nephew Cholmley Turner sixty-six years later in 1742, in the currently fashionable Classical style. The whole composition echoes Wren's much larger works at Chelsea and Greenwich, and is laid out as a rectangular courtyard, open on the northern side and separated from the rest of the village by a magnificent wrought-iron screen and entrance gates with the founder's arms in the arched overthrow (see Figure 9 and Plate 9). As at Chelsea, the central portion of the main southern range is occupied by an imposing chapel with lofty tower and cupola and flanked on both sides by schoolrooms, one for boys and one for girls. The two remaining ranges comprise the accommodation for the pensioners, originally men on the western side and women in the eastern, characterised by two statues, one of each sex, set high up in niches in the first floor façades, the representatives of each dressed in the distinctive gowns of the period. Now there is little distinction between the occupiers of the two ranges since the schoolrooms have been converted into residential accommodation during the interim period.

Finally, there are the foundations of the townspeople themselves,

Fig 8. Plan of Newarke Hospital, Leicester, Leicestershire.

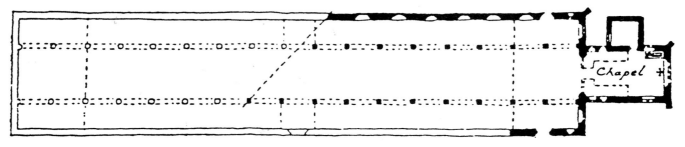

together with those of the guilds and trade associations, as well as the quasi-public organisations such as Trinity House.

As mentioned earlier, most mediaeval towns could boast at least one or two hospitals either for travellers or for the aged and infirm. Beverley has already been alluded to, as has York, the site of the largest mediaeval hospital in the land. As York was such an important centre, second only to London in status, it is not surprising that the merchant guilds there played an important part in the city's life. Many of the mediaeval guildhalls of London were destroyed during the Great Fire. York was more fortunate in that four of its halls, the centres for the guilds' administration and ceremonial, have been retained. The undercrofts of two of these were used as hospitals for the guilds' aged members.

The fourteenth century Merchant Venturers' Hall, perhaps the best known, is situated in Fossgate and is surrounded on three sides by a garden of rest from which the undercroft hospital and its adjoining chapel can be seen (see Plate 10). Less well-known is St. Anthony's Hall which dates from the fifteenth century, and is situated at Peasholm Green. Once again, the hospital undercroft is easily recognisable. Both buildings are open to visitors during certain specified hours, the former as a tourist attraction in its own right and the latter as part of the university library.

Finally, Newcastle-upon-Tyne, the largest city in the north of England displays all the characteristics of a regional capital which has happily been exempt from the interference of aristocratic government down the years. It retains three great almshouses provided by the townspeople themselves.

The Holy Jesus Hospital (see Plate 11) in City Road was built around 1682 according to an indenture dated 20th March 1683:

"...by the Mayor and burgesses of Newcastle-upon-Tyne for the maintenance, subtentation and relief of poor impotent people, being Freemen and Freemen's widows or their sons and daughters that have never been married, for ever, and that the inmates should be incorporated

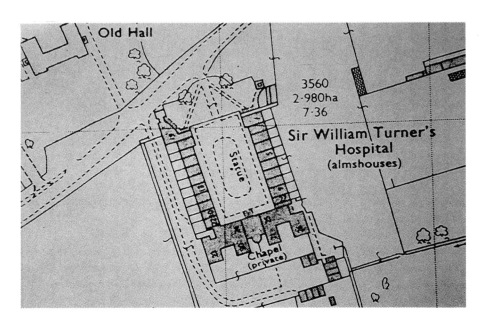

Fig 9. Plan of Kirkleatham Hospital, Cleveland.

by the name of Master, Brethren and Sisters of the Hospital of Holy Jesus, to have a common seal with a cross graven thereon, and in the circumference Sigillium Hospitalis Sanoti Jesu in Novo Castro".

By this indenture the mayor, aldermen and common council of the city were made the trustees with the rules of the hospital being adopted at the council meeting of 16th April 1683.

Later in the eighteenth century, three other hospitals were built by the Corporation alongside Holy Jesus. They were: Ann Davison's Hospital of 1719, founded under the terms of her will for the relief of the widows of poor Protestant clergymen, merchants and freemen of the town; Thomas Davison's Hospital of 1754 for six unmarried women, daughters or widows of burgesses; and Sir Walter Blackett's Hospital also of 1754 founded for six unmarried men. All three hospitals were demolished ninety-three years later to make way for the railway.

Holy Jesus Hospital fell into disrepair in the 1920s and the charity itself was relocated to a site elsewhere in the city centre, in Spital Tongues. The building remained unused and in danger of being demolished until 1967 when a determined effort by a joint working group of interested bodies, together with the director of the city's museums, resulted in the building being converted into a local history museum. It has remained as such since 1971 and is currently open to visitors six days a week.

The second great almshouse in Newcastle, but unlike Holy Jesus still in active residential use, is the Keelmen's Hospital also situated in City Road, some two hundred yards or so to the east of Holy Jesus.

In the late 1600s, there was a trend in Newcastle as elsewhere for societies and groups of tradesmen to band together to help their poor brethren. The keelmen were just such a society, being the guild of merchant seamen involved particularly in the shipping of coal.

Although coalminers lived mainly in the villages in Northumberland and County Durham, the keelmen lived in the town, in the crowded quarter of Sandgate on The Quayside. (The first line of the folk song "The Keelrow" begins "As I came thro' Sandgate"). They had charge of the lighters, or keels as they were called, which carried coal from the river to sea-going colliers. A keel was usually propelled by oars, but sometimes by a small square sail, and had a crew of two men and a boy. In 1600 there were eighty-five keels on the Tyne; today there are none.

Keelmen were a breed apart; most of them originated from the cattle-thieving tribes on both sides of the Border. They tended to intermarry and kept their own company and customs. A keelman's dress was quite distinctive; a yellow waistcoat and a white shirt filling the gap between light grey bell-bottom trousers and a blue jacket. Round his neck he wore a black silk handkerchief and on his head a black felt hat with ribbons.

By fixing levies, the society was at first able to raise money for relief, but strong feelings in favour of building a permanent hospital motivated them to erect such a building which was completed in 1701.

At first the keelmen charged a levy of four pence each tide they worked (known as the keelmen's groat) to maintain the hospital. In 1730 they formed a benefit society and in 1788 Parliament passed an Act:

"...establishing a permanent fund for the relief and support of skippers and Keelmen employed on the River Tyne, who by sickness or other accidental misfortune, or by old age, shall not be able to maintain themselves and their families, and for the relief of widows and children of such skippers and keelmen."

The fifty-five dwellings are situated around an enclosed courtyard with access in the centre of each side (see figure 10). The whole building is on an eminence at the eastern end of the Quayside affording magnificent views over the Tyne and its famous bridges (see Plate 12).

Also connected with the river and its traffic, the Trinity House Almshouses are situated in Broad Chare, adjoining the Maritime Museum in the Quayside area. The Corporation of Trinity House was founded in Deptford, London in about 1514 as the Guild of Holy Trinity and St. Clement, its patron being no less a person than Henry VIII. It is the general lighthouse and pilotage authority for England and Wales and is represented on harbour boards and similar bodies concerned with shipping. Because of its connection with the Navy the guild was spared by Henry when other religious organisations were seized, but as a precaution against future threats it changed its name to the Corporation of Trinity House of Deptford and Strond, securing confirmation of its charter under that name in 1547.

Most ports have Trinity House personnel, particularly river pilots, and Newcastle is no exception. Down the years the charity like other guilds sought ways to support its retired members, and between 1787 and 1791 provided a small group of almshouses with chapel and master's rooms around a small courtyard just off The Quayside proper. Finally, St. Mary's Hospital, founded before 1189, was originally situated in Westgate, providing accommodation initially for a master and six brethren.

Following a decree of the High Court of Chancery in 1840, the income of the charity was divided more or less equally between the brethren, the remuneration of the master and the foundation of two schools, one for boys and one for girls. The almshouses were later transferred to a site further out of the city centre and the site redeveloped, the only part remaining in Westgate being the gatepost which was incorporated into the fabric of the new development.

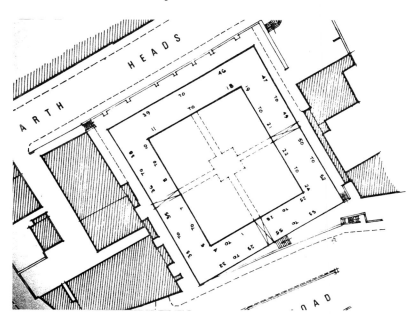

Fig 10. Plan of the Keelmen's Hospital, Newcastle-upon-Tyne, Tyne and Wear.

Plate 5. Hospital of B. V.
Beverley, Humberside.

Plate 6. The Commandery,
Hospital of St Wulston,
Worcester, Hereford and
Worcester.

Plate 7. Interior of St. Leonard's Hospital, York, North Yorkshire.

Plate 8. Beamsley Hospital, Craven after renovation.

Plate 9. *Kirkleatham Hospital, Cleveland.*

Plate 10. *Merchant Venturers' Hospital, York, North Yorkshire.*

Plate 11. Holy Jesus Hospital, Newcastle-upon-Tyne, Tyne and Wear.

Plate 12. The Keelmen's Hospital, Newcastle-upon-Tyne, Tyne and Wear.

Chapter 3

Mediaeval
Hospital Buildings

As mentioned earlier, the forerunner of the mediaeval hospital was the monastic farmery which, having been developed from an ordinary dorter or dormitory into a special ward for sick and infirm monks, was extended in scope, firstly for sick and later for elderly poor people.

The very early hospitals were ordinary private domestic buildings which were extended and adapted for their new purpose. Indeed, a few of the lazer houses, notably Harbledown near Canterbury, founded by Lanfranc the first Archbishop of Canterbury, were just a collection of huts or cottages with an ordinary chapel, clustered around a green enclosure.

Lanfranc's other foundation, the Hospital of St. John also at Canterbury, was much more substantial. The historian Eadmer who was alive during the period when it was founded (before 1098) described it thus:

"...he (Lanfranc) built a fair, large house of stone, and added to it several habitations for the various needs and conveniences of the men, together with an ample plot of ground."

Although fragments of these early buildings remain in some of the chapels which have fortunately come down to us as parish churches, our only real archive from which we can obtain details of the various building types is the collection of hospital seals, which have survived together with a few primitive sketches unearthed in contemporary manuscripts. Some of the seals are remarkably detailed. Figure 11 illustrates three. The first, that of St. John's Hospital, Exeter, built during the thirteenth century, clearly shows the church-like building with an arcade of round arches along the nave and a roof of ornamental shingles; the second, of the Hospital of St. Alexis, Exeter also of the thirteenth century, shows a somewhat larger building with clerestory arcading, again under a shingle roof. Both buildings were obviously substantial stone-built structures built by professionals. The third seal, slightly different from the other two, attempts to portray the hospital building of St. John's, Stafford, in three dimensions. This hospital was also clearly a substantial building, again with a church-like exterior. The architectural features, halfway between the Early English and Decorated styles, depict triple lancet windows with a delicately pierced trefoil above and arcading running round the entire ground floor.

It is difficult to appreciate just what a prodigious output of building took place during the early Middle Ages, when the population of the entire country was less than five million people; castles, manor houses, monasteries, cathedrals and the majority of the country's 12,000 parish churches, as well as all the usual domestic and agricultural buildings. Moreover, during the pre-Reformation period alone, between the twelfth and sixteenth centuries, something of the order of eight hundred hospitals were erected. Such studies of hospital buildings that have been carried out by antiquarians, notably the Victorian architect, F.T.Dolman, cite four distinct building types, each one a development of its predecessor, and all of them owing their lineage to monastic prototypes. They were, in chronological order: 1. Great Hall with chapel attached. 2. Great Hall with chapel detached.

Fig 11. Hospital Seals.

39

3. The cruciform layout. 4. Narrow courtyard.

The first two, with or without direct access to the adjoining chapel, will be dealt with in the remainder of this chapter. The other two, being essentially transitional in character, between the original concept of a hospital and the emerging design of self-contained almshouses, will be covered in later chapters.

Great Hall with chapel attached

This was the most direct descendant of the monastic farmery. It was single-storeyed in its earliest form and its basic design was epitomised by St. Mary's Hospital, Chichester, which was founded in about 1229 upon the site of a defunct nunnery. Figure 12 shows the typical ground plan of this hospital with the chapel built as an extension to the hall, although in this particular case it is thought that the chapel preceded the latter. The great hall originally of six bays, truncated to four sometime in the early sixteenth century, is covered with a massive trussed rafter roof, some forty-two feet to the ridge, which sweeps almost to ground level over the side aisles which form the individual cubicles for the eight inmates. Figure 13 shows a section through the building, after Dolman, with a small vignette showing a perspective from the south-east.

The plan of the Hospital of St. Nicholas, Salisbury (Figure 14) is a variation on the basic design, this time a double hospital with both the hall and the chapel at the eastern end divided into two, longitudinally, by arcading. This hospital, thought to have been the model for Hiram's Hospital in Trollope's novel *The Warden*, was founded as early as 1214.

A further variation on the theme of a double hospital is that of St. John the Baptist, Winchester (Figure 15) where the chapel was built in 1290, as an extension of the southern infirmary hall.

Yet another, although a more conventional variation on the basic design, is Bishop Bubwith's Hospital of St. Saviour, Wells, founded in 1424, again as a double house for twelve men and twelve women. The chapel is built as usual at the eastern end, whilst at the other extremity was situated the city's guildhall, now also used as almshouses (Figure 16 and Plate 13).

Founded one year earlier than Wells in 1423, by Henry Chichele, Archbishop of Canterbury, the Bede House at Higham Ferrers, Northamptonshire, is generally thought to have replaced an earlier hospital dedicated to St. James, since fragments of that building have been incorporated into the fabric of the current building. Archbishop Chichele endowed

Fig 12. Plan of St. Mary's Hospital, Chichester, West Sussex.

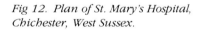

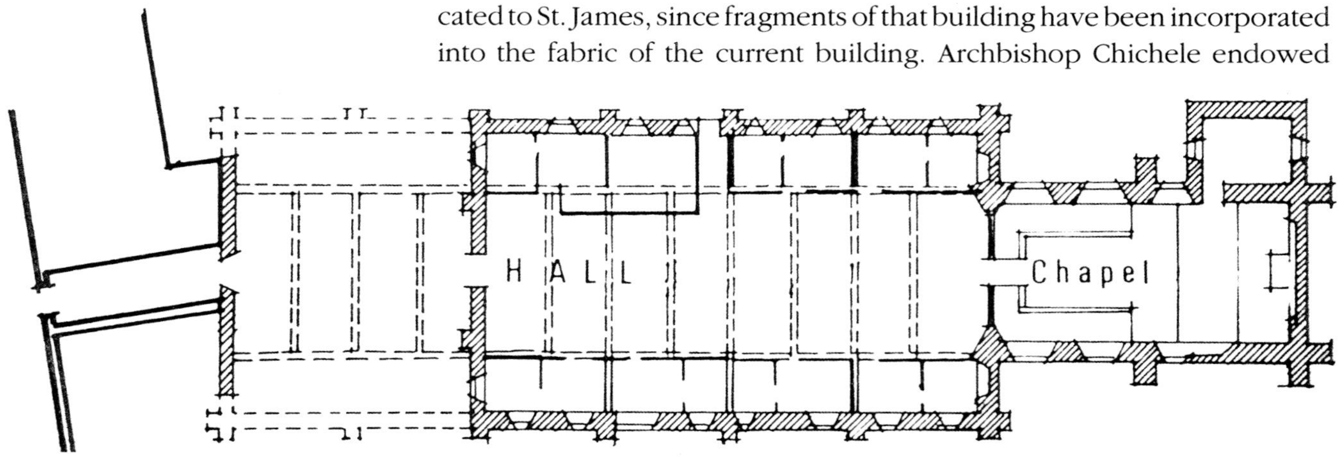

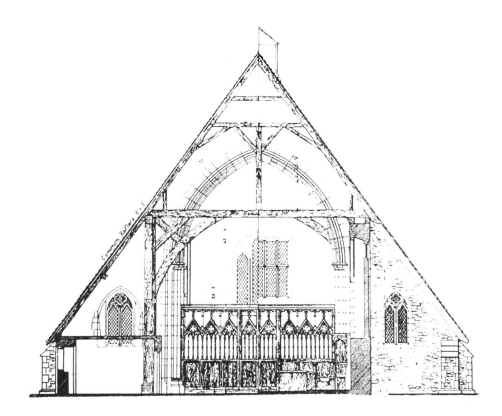

Fig 13. Section through St. Mary's Hospital, Chichester, West Sussex.

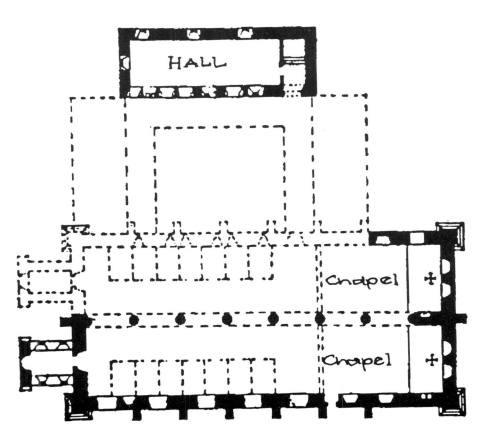

Fig 14. Plan of St. Nicholas' Hospital, Salisbury, Wiltshire.

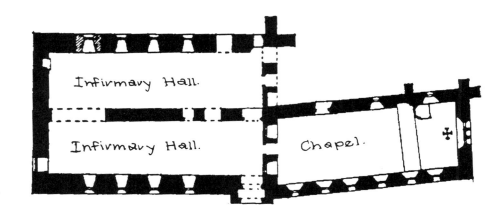

Fig 15. Plan of Hospital of St. John the Baptist, Winchester, Hampshire.

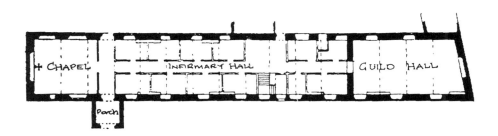

Fig 16. Plan of Bishop Bubwith's Hospital, Wells, Somerset.

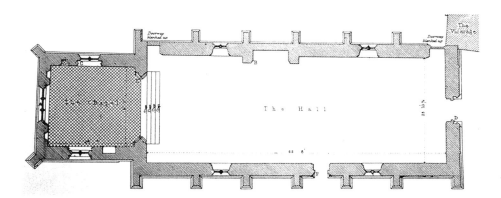

Fig 17. Plan of the Bede House, Higham Ferrers, Northamptonshire.

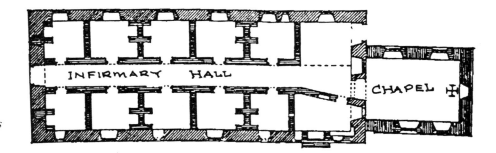

Fig 18. Plan of St. Mary Magdalene's Hospital, Glastonbury, Somerset.

three institutions in his native town, a college, a school and the Bede House. Only the last two mentioned institutions survive. The Bede House follows the conventional plan of hall with chapel opening from it at the eastern end (see Figure 17 and Plate 14). Its striking features are the alternate courses of red and cream stone of which the walls are constructed, together with a central fireplace with five-centred arch around which the twelve male inmates and their nurse would have been likely to gather on chilly evenings. The buildings fell into disrepair in the late Middle Ages, the bedesmen having become out-pensioners, but were restored in the 1850s and are now used as a Sunday School.

Finally, we have an example of a hospital which has been converted into self-contained almshouses, that of St. Mary Magdalene, Glastonbury, another institution founded in the thirteenth century. From this plan (Figure 18), the original hospital form can be seen with the chapel in the usual place at the eastern end. However, instead of the usual cubicles, the hall has been divided into eleven self-contained, two-storey dwellings with access from the central corridor. Unfortunately, only one half of this important almshouse remains.

Some hospital buildings like St. Mary Magdalene, Glastonbury were converted to two or more storeys sometime after they had been built, and the Newarke Hospital, Leicester referred to in the previous chapter had a further floor inserted during the seventeenth century. There were others which were constructed with two storeys from the very beginning which were generally founded towards the end of the pre-Reformation period, during the fifteenth and very early sixteenth centuries. The most conventional, bearing the greatest similarity to the original design, was the hospital of St. John the Baptist and St. John the Evangelist at Sherborne, Dorset (Figure 19). Founded in 1437 by the townspeople of Sherborne after a quarrel with Sherborne Abbey deprived them of the use of the

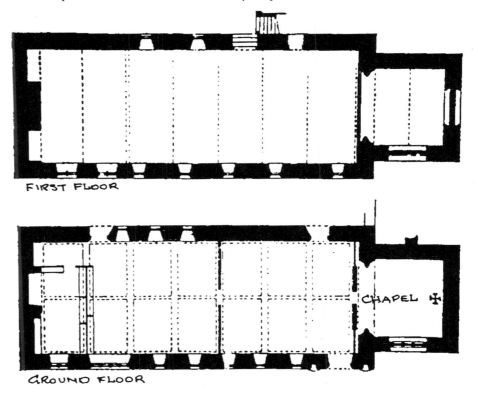

Fig 19. Plan of Hospital of SS. John the Evangelist / Baptist, Sherborne, Dorset.

monastic hospital, the hospital housed six men on the ground floor and six women on the upper, the latter being reached via an external stair with both sexes having access to the diminutive chapel at the altar rail situated at the eastern end of each floor.

Great Hall with chapel detached

Lanfranc, in building his hospital of St. John at Canterbury some time before 1089, designed it for patients of both sexes, thirty men and thirty women in a double hospital with a long hall, 150 feet by 28 feet wide, divided into two halves (Figure 20). At right angles to this hall, again divided into two, longitudinally this time, was the chapel, each half having a separate altar in order that men and women could worship separately. Very little is left of the building other than its famous timber gatehouse (Plate 15), but from what remains it would appear that access to the chapel was taken directly from the hall.

Founded in 1158, St. Mary Magdalene, Winchester, again with de-tached chapel but this time separated from the hospital proper by the master's dwelling, provides perhaps the most complete plan of a lazer-house which has come down to us. The buildings remained until 1788, the plan being recorded in Vetusta Monumenta (Figure 21), showing a row of cells on the east-west axis, with the chapel on the south-eastern end. The side opposite to the church is thought to have been occupied by a common hall, although no details of that exist. The whole building was destroyed in the early nineteenth century, although the Norman doorway was moved to a building in Peter Street.

Finally, perhaps the most complete example of this type of hospital in existence, is that dedicated to St. John the Baptist in Northampton (Figure 22 and Plate 16). There is some confusion as to the origins of this building. According to the historian, Leland, the hospital was founded by William Sancte Clere, Archdeacon of Northampton in 1327, although there is documentary evidence pointing to its existence 189 years earlier as having been erected for the reception of infirm poor by Archdeacon Walter. The hospital had endowments throughout Northamptonshire and elsewhere, amounting in 1555 to £51.19s.6d, although nine years later, at the date of the suppression of chantries and hospitals, it was valued only at £25.6s.2d.

From the disposition of the hall relative to the chapel, it would seem that this was not the first such building. Rather, it appears that as is usual with early hospitals, the original hall was situated to the west of the chapel. However, as the old idea of a general hospital, accessible to all for short periods, gave way to permanent accommodation for almspeople, the original hall was removed and replaced in the fourteenth century by a residential hall on adjoining land. Because of this, direct access was curtailed and the pensioners thereafter had to use a side door.

The hospital was administered by a master who, unusually, was not necessarily a clergyman, assisted by two co-brothers or chaplains. The master appointed the co-brothers, he himself being appointed by the Bishop of Lincoln. The two chaplains lived on the premises, in rooms above the first floor of the hospital building, whilst the master lived in a house nearby.

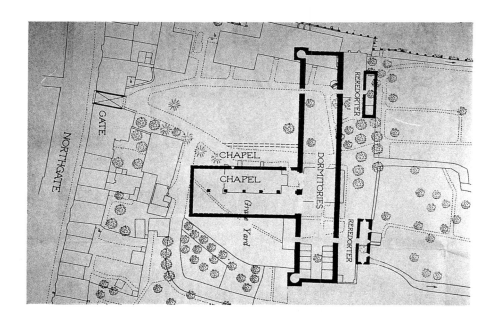

Fig 20. Plan of the Hospital of St. John, Canterbury, Kent.

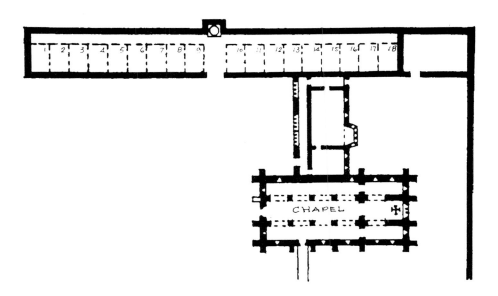

Fig 21. Plan of Hospital of St. Mary Magdalene, Winchester, Hampshire.

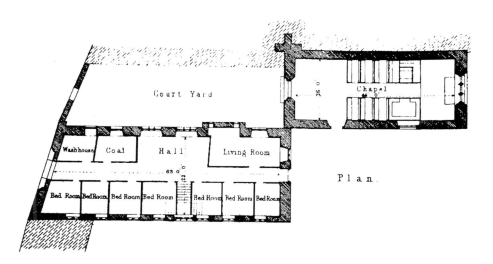

Fig 22. Plan of Hospital of St. John the Baptist, Northampton, Northamptonshire.

The gradual change in the purpose of hospitals from general care of the sick and infirm to permanent accommodation for the elderly was accelerated by the dissolution of religious houses under Henry VIII and Edward VI, and resulted in many newly formed institutions using the local parish church for worship instead of having their own chapels.

This period of transition produced many great almshouses, some of which will be examined in detail in the next chapter. Before doing so however, we must consider one further hospital which although founded in the late Norman period, went through many vicissitudes during the ensuing eight hundred years. It now exhibits most, if not all of the features discussed in the present chapter.

The Great Hospital of St. Giles, Norwich was founded by Walter de Suffield, Bishop of Norwich in 1249 for a master, four chaplains, a deacon, sub-deacon and four sisters to minister to thirteen poor people and seven poor scholars. The original plan (Figure 23), different from any described so far, was monastic in concept, the main buildings surrounding a cloister garth, some 50 feet square. Unlike most monasteries the conventual buildings were situated on the northern, rather than the southern side of the church. The infirmary hall only now some four bays long with aisles (although the southern one is now missing), lies to the south of the cloisters and to the west of the diminutive parish church of St. Helen, which was included in the precincts because the founding bishop demolished the original church building when the hospital was erected. The chancel to the east of St. Helen's, although designated as the hospital chapel, was used by the chaplains whose dormitory lay to the north of the cloisters adjoining the master's lodgings. Both these buildings have since been replaced with almshouse dwellings. The in-pensioners' hall lies to the west of the cloisters whilst the eastern side was occupied by the chapter house, long since gone except for its western wall.

The original hospital was dissolved by Henry VIII, but following a petition by the townspeople of Norwich, it was refounded by Edward VI

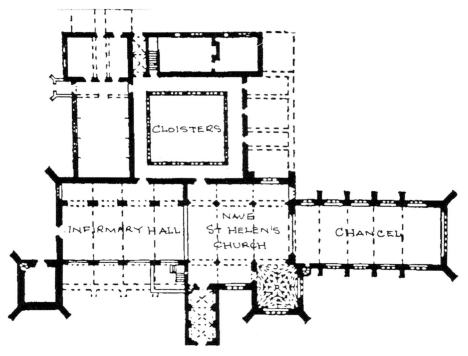

Fig 23. Plan of the Great Hospital, Norwich, Norfolk.

(1537-53) in 1553 when its character was altered and further wards inserted at first floor level in the hall and the chancel, reached by external staircases. The residential accommodation was at this time separated from the parish church by solid walls, necessitating access for worship being taken from the cloisters or through a long vaulted porch from the road. Since its second foundation several groups of cottages have been added and the hospital now supports over 200 almspeople, both in and out-pensioners.

Plate 13. Bishop Bubwith's Hospital, Wells, Somerset.

Plate 14. The Bede House, Higham Ferrers, Northants.

Plate 15. The Gatehouse, Hospital of St. John, Canterbury, Kent.

Plate 16. Hospital of St. John the Baptist, Northampton, Northants.

Chapter 4

The Transition
to the Almshouse

England is by no means the only country where the erection of hospitals and almshouses has been undertaken.

As mentioned in the opening chapter, the main impetus for the building of British monastic institutions came after the Norman Conquest. For centuries before that, many conventual establishments both large and small had been founded abroad, firstly throughout Eastern Europe following the beginnings of monasticism in the more remote corners of the Holy Land, and later spreading to Western Europe, where particularly the Rules of the Augustinian and Cistercian Orders were codified.

As in England, the designs of the earliest hospitals on the Continent were based upon monastic models, but in Italy particularly, with its dominance by the Papal See, the increasing sizes of these establishments in the sixteenth centuries necessitated a review of administrative practices and a complete rethink of their designs. From this emerged the Cruciform and Courtyard layout.

The Cruciform Layout

Before the sixteenth century, the two most important Italian hospitals were situated in Florence and Sienna. In 1546 the architect Filarate, in addition to being the sculptor responsible for the bronze gates of St. Peter's in Rome, was asked to design a hospital to bring together under one roof the numerous charities which existed at the time in Milan. He studied all the contemporary buildings of the type, and his Ospidale Maggiore successfully resolved the combined secular and religious needs of the charitable institutions by providing ranges of buildings round a series of interconnected courtyards (Figure 24). This design was widely used throughout Italy and Spain; at the Hospital of Santo Spirito in Sassio in Rome, and at Santiago de Compostela (1499), Granada (1504), Tavera, Toledo (1540) and Santa Cruz, Toledo (1501) in Spain.

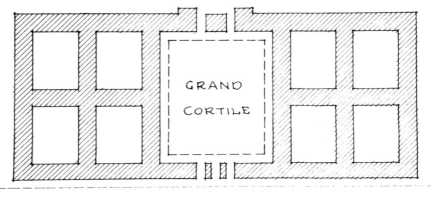

Fig 24. Plan of Ospidale Maggiore, Milan, Italy.

The plan of the Hospital of Santa Cruz at Toledo, designed by Enrique Egan, and reproduced at Figure 25 is typical of the slightly smaller hospital based upon the cruciform plan, a derivation of the original infirmary hall. This plan form allowed four large wards to be conjoined at the crossing where the altar, visible to all was provided, generally under a tower. Originally four cloister courts were planned, one at each corner with conjoined wards forming two of the four sides of each, but in the event only two were built.

Only one hospital of this type is known to have been erected in England; that endowed by Henry VII (1457-1509) in 1503 on the north bank of the River Thames in London at The Savoy (Figure 26). The original building on the site was the Savoy Palace, which had been totally destroyed by a rampaging mob in 1381. Before commissioning the building of this hospital, the king made extensive enquiries into contemporary practices concerning the design and running of hospitals abroad, as can be ascertained from a remarkable document in the Bodleian Library at Oxford, which gives a long and detailed account – specially commissioned by the king – of the hospital in Florence by its master, Francis Portinary. The king superintended the building's design:

"We have begoune to erecte, buylde and establisshe a commune Hospital... and the same we intend with Godd's grace to finish, after the maner, fourme and fashion of a plat which is devised for the same, and signed with our hande."

The Savoy Hospital was completed in 1519 when a master and four chaplains were appointed and beds for one hundred poor people were provided. Apparently no cloisters as such were built, although a cemetery was provided to the north-west, between the hospital buildings and the church of St. Mary le Savoy which still exists. The hospital was suppressed

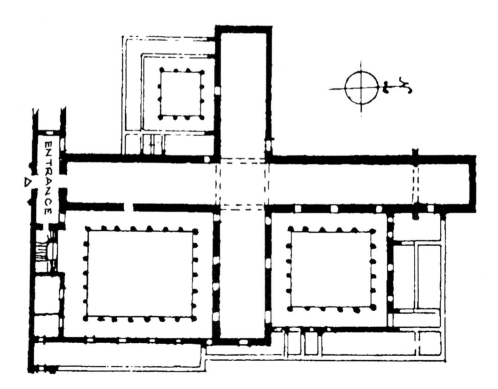

Fig 25. Plan of the Hospital of Santa Cruz, Toledo, Spain.

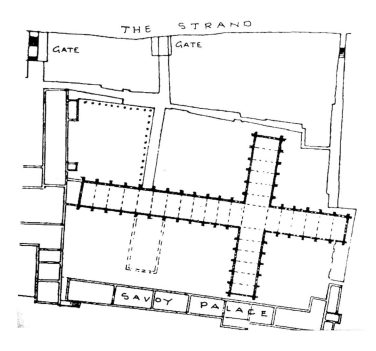

Fig 26. Plan of the Savoy Hospital, London.

by Henry's grandson Edward VI in 1555, only to be reinstated by Queen Mary, although by the time of her death the mastership had become a sinecure. The hospital was demolished in 1553, but the chapel remains in Savoy Street off The Strand.

The Courtyard Design

The true cruciform hospital was large and extravagant in the use of land with each of the four cloisters having buildings on two adjacent sides only, and the other two open to view. It did not take long, however, for someone to realise that by moving the four bays around one cloister garth, much less land was involved. The building was architecturally more satisfying, there was much more privacy for the occupants and the whole undertaking was easier to manage. As a result, the courtyard form was adopted as the most common type of development for almshouses during the next five hundred years or so, with generally two variations on the theme, totally enclosed with pedestrian access only or open on one side with a screen wall with gate and railings to restrict vehicular access. The courtyard design also became popular in many kinds of religious and educational establishments, notably at the universities of Oxford and Cambridge, and just as the infirmary hall plan had dominated the early mediaeval period, so the courtyard design dominated the post-Reformation years and continued to do so, with modifications, until Victorian times.

All manner of charities can trace their origins back to early monasticism; many educational establishments, schools, colleges and universities, and of course almshouse charities themselves. However, the sixteenth century was a particularly fruitful period for such foundations, and it was during this time when the mediaeval craft guilds were at their most influential that many more hospitals were founded, most of them for the care of the aged, but increasingly, as the century bore on, also as charity schools for the education of the children of the poor. Some of these have survived as the great public schools of today.

To start with, many of these newly formed hospitals provided for both the young and the old; in many cases the hospitals were founded by wealthy guild masters to provide, on the one hand for the needs of old and decayed members in their declining years, and on the other for the sons and daughters of less fortunate guildsmen, feeding, clothing, housing them and educating them generally for a life similar to that of their parents. But in later centuries the establishments became more specialised, by either taking on the whole function of an almshouse and dropping the educational role, or vice versa.

A classic example of the latter is Christ's Hospital, London which was originally founded during the reign of Edward VI by Bishop Ridley, to provide not solely education, but complete maintenance for destitute children and infants, as well as out-relief for the aged. The hospital was supported entirely by the citizens of London and by a royal grant. Edward actually signed its charter on his death bed in 1552. However, very early on in its history it ceased to cater for the elderly altogether, concentrating instead on education and went on to become one of the most prestigious schools in the country.

Another, less well-known example is Bond's or Bablake's Hospital in Coventry, founded in 1507 by Thomas Bond, sometime Mayor of Coventry, for the care and maintenance of ten poor men of the Trinity and Corpus Christi Guilds. Some fifty years later another institution was founded alongside by the Corporation for the maintenance and instruction of poor boys. The two charities lived happily side by side into the twentieth century, the old hospital being known as Bablake's (Plate 17) and the new one as Bond's. The two hospital buildings form the north and east sides of a small quadrangle (Figure 27). The west side is occupied by a later master's house and the south by the churchyard of the original guild's church, now the parish church of St. John. Incidentally, in 1647 this was where several hundred prisoners from the defeated Scottish army of the

Fig 27. Plan of Bablake's and Bond's Hospitals, Coventry, West Midlands.

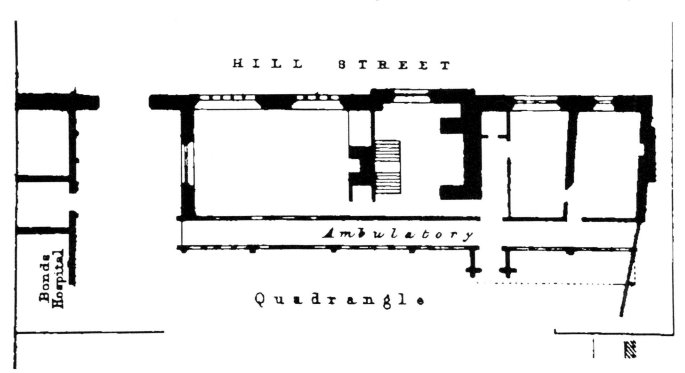

54

Duke of Hamilton were billeted. The citizens boycotted the prisoners and it is from this episode that the expression "sent to Coventry" is supposed to have originated.

Many of these new institutions adopted the new collegiate or court-yard form of development; that is to say buildings were erected on all four sides of a rectangular open space with access for pedestrians only through archways at ground floor level, usually in the centre of each range, although very occasionally they were provided at the corners.

The open space varied in size from extremely small courts around which from eight to a dozen dwellings were situated, to large imposing compositions of up to a hundred or more almshouses with master's lodgings, church or chapel, communal hall and sometimes an audit or committee room where the trustees conducted the formal business of the charity. Perhaps the best example of a small to medium size almshouse of this type is that at Ewelme, a few miles to the south-west of Oxford.

William de la Pole, sometime Earl of Suffolk, together with his wife, Alice, a grand-daughter incidentally of Geoffrey Chaucer (1340-1400), founded this hospital together with the adjoining free school in 1437. King Henry VI (1421-71) granted the couple a charter for the purpose:

" ..that they or either of them should found an hospital at their manor at Ewelme, in the county of Oxford and settle a sufficient endowment not exceeding two hundred marks for the maintenance of two chaplains and thirteen poor men to be incorporated and to have a common seal."

and further:

" ..that the above number of persons should be ever maintained in it, one of the chaplains of the Almshouse, who shall govern it and shall administer the affairs thereof."

William de la Pole, by this time having been elevated to a dukedom, made final provision for the endowment of the charity in his will dated 1448. This was only just in time, however, since he fell out of favour with the Establishment and was beheaded one year later. Alice continued to maintain the almshouses under the terms of her husband's will, living to a great age. She died in 1475 and was buried in the parish church which adjoins and connects with the almshouses that she herself had caused to be built after her husband's untimely demise.

Upon the attainder of one of William's descendants, the Earl of Lincoln, during the reign of Henry VIII, the Suffolk estates were forfeit to the Crown, when the manor of Ewelme became a royal manor. Early in the reign of James I (1566-1625) the rectory and the canonry of Christ Church was vested in the Professorship of Divinity at Oxford and in 1617 the mastership of the hospital went to the Regius Professorship of Physic at the same university. Both appointments continue to this day.

Figure 28 shows a plan of the entire complex, church, almshouses and school. The church is situated upon the higher ground with its tower dominating the village. Further down the slope, to the west end of the church and connected to it by a passage and a short flight of steps, lie the homes of the almsfolk, occupying four sides of a quadrangle, approximately fifty feet by fifty feet, each dwelling consisting of a sitting-room on the ground floor with a bedroom over. A covered ambulatory or cloister extends all round the quadrangle in front of the dwellings. The steeply pitched shingle roof, which was at one time thatched, sweeps down over the cloisters, with small dormer windows obtruding into the roof-scape, providing illumination to the tiny bedrooms. In the centre of each side of the ambulatory, a clerestoried and gabled entrance gives access to the cloister-garth in the centre of which stands an ancient pump, from which in times gone by, the almsfolk drew their water. The external walls of the dwellings are of stone to match the church, although the frontages to the courtyard are of brick, thought by some historians to be one of the first uses of this material for domestic buildings in the country. The oak uprights and herring-bone brick spandrels are a distinctive and characteristic feature of this type of construction in Oxfordshire.

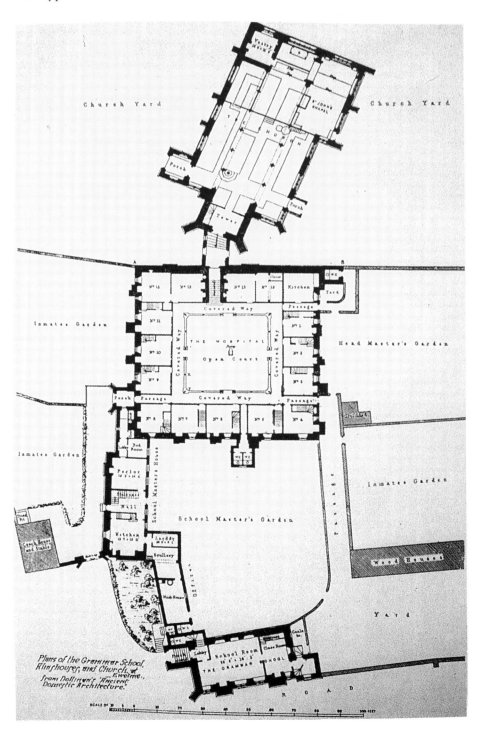

Fig 28. Plan of Ewelme Hospital, Oxfordshire.

Over the west side of the courtyard and, owing to the rapid fall of the land down from west to east, almost at the same level as the church, are the audit and muniment rooms and a suite of accommodation originally provided for the schoolmaster. These were used in times gone by for the administration of the hospital's affairs, but have since been converted for the use of the almsfolk. At the bottom of the slope is situated the free grammar school, separated from the hospital by the under-schoolmaster's house and an entrance porch, a picturesque brick-built structure of great charm.

The whole composition forms a most interesting example of mediaeval domestic architecture, combining as it does provision for the public offices and ministrations of the church, the comfort of a home for the aged and needy and a place of instruction for the village children (Plate 18).

Another, much larger collegiate type almshouse, St. Cross Hospital, was established in 1136 near Winchester by Henry de Blois, brother to King Stephen and Bishop of Winchester. In those days its plan form would have been that of the conventional infirmary block, with presumably the usual chapel attached.

Thirteen "impotent poor men" were to be maintained permanently in the hospital and provided with lodging, suitable raiment and sufficient food. This was stipulated to be a daily allowance of a loaf of bread, three pounds and four ounces in weight, a gallon and a half of small beer, together with a pottage composed of milk and bread called mortrel and wastel, and a dish of flesh or fish according to the day of the week and the season, with further supplies for supper.

In addition to the thirteen occupants, provision was made for a hundred other poor men "of good conduct of the more indigent classes", to be maintained as out-pensioners, each receiving daily a loaf of bread and three quarts of small beer. A special building was erected for this purpose in the outer curia, called the "hundred mennes hall", much of which remains to this day.

There was in addition a foundation for a master, a steward, four chaplains, thirteen clerks, seven choristers, who were to be educated in the hospital, and sundry servants. The comptrollers or administrators of the charity, appointed by Henry de Blois, were the Hospitallers of St. John of Jerusalem, the Knights Hospitallers, who had a Preceptory at Baddesly near Lymington in Hampshire. The appointment of the prior or master was vested in the Bishop of Winchester and the rents and other endowments, among which were several parish churches in Hampshire and elsewhere, were to be enjoyed by the hospital forever.

After Henry de Blois had died, a series of disputes concerning the administration of the affairs of the hospital broke out between his successor as Bishop of Winchester, Richard de Toclyve and the Knights Hospitaller, which resulted in the intervention of the king, Henry II (1132-89), who finally decreed that the hospital should be under the total control of the bishop and his successors. In 1185 Bishop Toclyve added a further hundred out-pensioners, but the income was insufficient to provide all the necessary alms and there followed a century where funds were perverted from their original purposes and various appointments were misapplied. In 1372 the government of the charity fell into the hands of William of

Wykeham, that prolific founder of educational establishments who, with great difficulty, recovered many of the institution's possessions, repaired the buildings and restored the system to its original order. He installed John de Campden as master, whose brass still exists in the floor of the church.

William Wykeham's immediate successor was Cardinal Beaufort, younger brother of Henry IV (1367-1413), who was responsible for the rebuilding and enlarging of the hospital and for the endowment of a second charity within its precincts, the House of Noble Poverty, an almshouse for decayed gentlemen. This second institution consisted of two priests, thirty-five brethren and three sisters, all under the master of the hospital and his successors. Cardinal Beaufort unfortunately died before all his plans could be fully commissioned and it was left to his successor William of Wayneflete, to procure the new charter from King Henry VI and complete the works. Later, during the Wars of the Roses, the endowment of the second charity was much reduced, so much so that the number of inmates had to be reduced to one chaplain and two brethren only.

The hospital was fortunate to escape the depredations of Henry VIII, but by the late seventeenth century the regulations for its government had been lost and the establishment was administered by custom only. Under the mastership of Rev. Dr. Abraham Markland a new code was drawn up called the *Consuetudinarium*, which with some modifications still continues to this day to be the governing instrument. Under its provisions, in addition to the inmates, then consisting of the master, one chaplain, one steward and thirteen brethren, twenty eight women and twelve men, all out-pensioners were to occupy the " hundred mennes hall". There were in addition, two other brethren termed "reversioners", who were to succeed on a death or vacancy. The master was to have authority over all persons belonging to the hospital and was empowered to receive all revenues from which he was to defray expenses and keep the buildings including the church in good repair. He was to keep the common seal of the hospital which was to be used on all leases and conveyances, appoint the steward and chaplain and in the event of any death or vacancy among the brethren or any in the "hundred mennes hall", appoint a replacement. Further, on the occurrence of any misdemeanour he was to have power to punish or even expel the offender. The brethren for their part were, on their admission, to take an oath of obedience to the master and the ordinances of the hospital and were required to be present at prayers twice each day. The steward was empowered to deputise for the master when he was away and the chaplain was, in addition to his clerical duties in the hospital, required to visit the sick in the adjoining parish.

The forty out-pensioners were allotted meat or soup with bread and a small allowance of money weekly. An allowance of bread and beer was also made for the purpose of giving alms at the gate to such poor persons who may claim the dole. There were also to be special doles six times during the year: Christmas Eve, Easter, the 3rd of May (the anniversary of the foundation of the hospital), the 10th of August (the anniversary of the founder's death) and the Eve of All Saints. On these days, distribution of small loaves was to be made to all applicants, a custom which still remains to this day. The *Consuetudinarium* was to be read publicly on the 3rd of May every year.

The general plan of the Hospital is shown in Figure 29 and the buildings illustrated in Plate 19.

Generally, the plan consists of two courtyards, interconnected by a monumental gatehouse. The smaller, the entrance court, gained from the road, is on the north side of the hospital. On the eastern side lies the "hundred mennes hall", now converted to other uses, and some modern buildings; to the west lie the kitchen and domestic quarters. On the fourth, the south side, is the noble gatehouse, erected by Cardinal Beaufort with its four-centred moulded archway with a coat of arms in each spandrel, that of the Crown to the right and that of the founder to the left. Over the doorway, in a niche stands the effigy of Cardinal Beaufort himself. Adjoining the gatehouse, between it and the kitchen, the remainder of the fourth side of the court has two of the windows of the hall, arch-headed with tracery and transom. The ceiling of the gatehouse is groined and on the left of the entrance lies the porter's lodge.

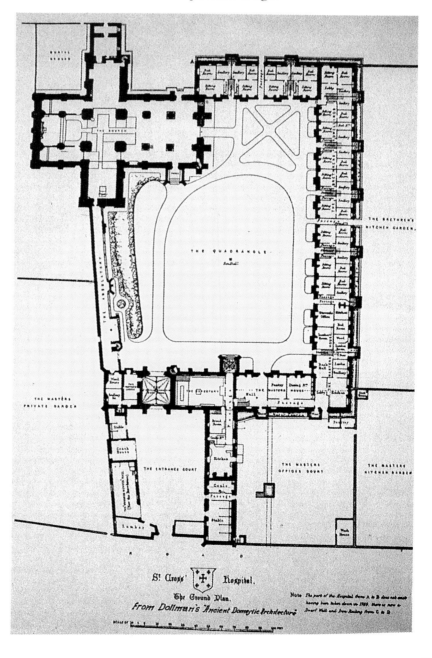

Fig 29. Plan of the Hospital of St. Cross, Winchester, Hampshire.

The larger inner court is magnificent. On the northern side is the gatehouse, the octagonal stair turret of which breaks up its otherwise symmetry and adjoining this lies the hall and the master's residence. The approach to the hall externally is via a flight of stairs and through a groined porch. On the east side lies a range of buildings consisting of a covered way connecting the gatehouse with the north entrance to the church. Over this is situated the hospital infirmary, from a window in which one can see the church altar.

The western side of the main court is occupied by the brethren's dwellings and these until 1789 were continued round the south side, abutting the church. Each dwelling consists of sitting-room, bedroom, scullery and a latrine for each inmate, discharging into a sluice on the western side of the range from the gabled projection. On this western side also lies the brethren's garden.

The brethren's dwellings on the courtyard side are extremely simple in design, consisting only of square-headed two-light and low, four-centred arched doorways, together with a series of projecting chimney stacks, rather like those at Vicars' Close, Wells.

To quote someone who in the mid-nineteenth century was describing the locale in which the hospital is situated:

"No one can pass its threshold without feeling himself landed, as it were, in another age. The ancient features of the building, the noble gateway, the quadrangle, the common refectory, the cloisters and, rising above all, the lofty and massive pile of the venerable church; the uniform garb and reverend mien of the aged brethren, the common provision for their declining years; the dole at the gatehouse, all lead back our thoughts to days when men gave their best to God's honour, and looked on what was done to his poor as done to Himself and were as lavish of architectural beauty on what modern habits might deem a receptacle for beggars, as on the noblest of royal palaces. It seems a place where no worldly thought, no pride or passion, or irreverence could enter; a spot where as a modern writer has beautifully expressed it, 'a good man, might he make his choice, would wish to die'."

In size as well as location, the tiny Spence's Hospital at Carleton-in-Craven on the southern fringes of the Yorkshire Dales, contrasts sharply with that of St. Cross. Founded in 1698 by Ferrand Spence, with additional endowment in 1872 by Agnes Vardill Niven, this almshouse must be among the smallest courtyard developments in the country, particularly one with dwellings on two floors with balcony access.

Originally the hospital consisted of twelve single-room dwellings with boardroom, built on three sides of a courtyard with open access gallery to the first floor, reached by two flights of steps, one on each side of the entrance gateway. Each dwelling's front door opens on to the court or gallery, with the windows facing outwards to views to the north, east and south. The remaining western side of the court consists of a fine stone gateway with ball finials and wrought-iron gates (Figure 30). In 1898 it was proposed to pull the buildings down and rebuild six separate dwellings, but this proposal was abandoned and a few years later, four water closets were installed, accessible from the covered passage downstairs and the gallery on the first floor.

In 1958 considerable improvements were carried out. The timbers of the gallery were replaced, new doors and windows and modern sinks were installed together with communal bathrooms, although the twelve separate rooms were retained.

Finally, in 1974 the whole hospital was refurbished to provide separate, self-contained dwellings consisting of a bed-sitting room, kitchen and bathroom. Perforce, the number of units was reduced to eight, although a warden's flat was provided by converting the boardroom. Apart from essential repairs, the exterior was hardly touched; each flat was provided with an extra window overlooking the courtyard to give interest value, and a small building to house the central-heating boiler was tucked away in a corner. All the fine stone chimney-stacks were retained, although only two flues are actually used. Plate 20 shows a view inside the courtyard. As a historic almshouse, it is a little gem; it is a little unfortunate, however, that

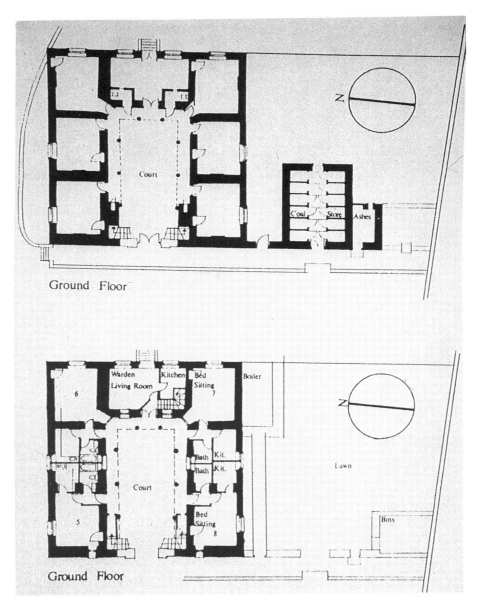

Fig 30. Plan of Spence's Hospital, Craven, North Yorkshire.

the trustees have decided to dispense with the name hospital, a venerable appellation, and have renamed the building, Spence's Court.

This section on courtyard design cannot be concluded without mention of two further almshouses of early foundation, both of national importance.

Browne's Hospital in Stamford, Lincolnshire, was founded in 1493, although it was refounded in 1610 when it consisted of a warden, confrater, ten poor men and two poor women "advancing in age". The hospital building proper, forming the south side of the courtyard, was of stone with handsome tower over, and of mediaeval style with cubicles against the outside walls and chapel at the eastern end. The warden's accommodation and nurses' kitchen formed a further two sides to the court, with the western end being enclosed by cloisters (Figure 31). Sadly,

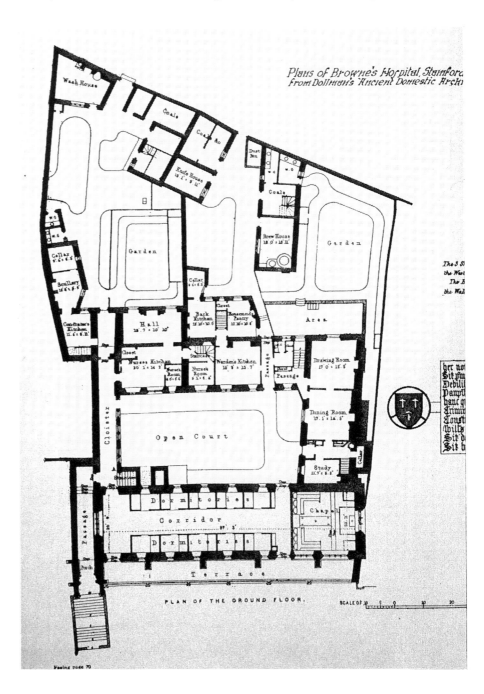

Fig 31. Plan of Browne's Hospital, Stamford, Lincolnshire.

the buildings on the northern side have been replaced with more modern dwellings (Plate 21) and the symmetry of the courtyard has suffered to a degree. However, the main building remains and is now used as a museum devoted to the history of almshouses.

Forde's delightful little hospital in the centre of Coventry was founded in 1529 and is one of the few half-timbered groups in the country. Originally, the foundation was for five poor men and one woman, the original inscription on the wall declaring:

"May the 4th, anno 1529, Mr William Fourd of this city, Merchant of the Staple, founded this almes-house for five men and one woman, and gave to each of them fivepence a week for their maintenance; afterwards Mr William Pisford, his executor, gave other lands, and appointed six men and their wives to be placed therein, and each couple to have seven pence half-penny a week, and the nurse the same. And in the room of the sixth poor man and his wife, there shall be one honest good woman of the said city

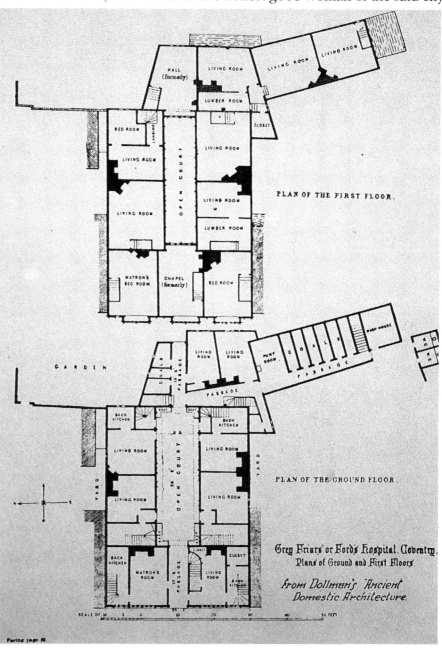

Fig 32. Plan of Forde's Hospital, Coventry, West Midlands.

taken into the Bede-house, which shall be about the age of forty, or betwix forty and fifty, to be the keeper of the said five poor men and their wives, as need shall require, to see them clean kept in their persons and houses, and for dressing their meat, washing of them, and ministering all things necessary to them."

The plan (Figure 32) consists of a narrow, open court, only some 40 feet long by 12 feet wide, entered at each end by a narrow doorway with five-centred arch over. The first floor jetties over, giving slightly more floor area to the upper dwellings compared with the ground floor, and leaving only some eight or nine feet between opposite living-room windows. However, since the Second World War, when the hospital was extensively damaged by enemy bombing, the building has been modernised and re-arranged internally to provide more comfortable and convenient accommodation for its occupants. Plate 22 shows the interior of the courtyard today.

Plate 17. Bablake's Hospital, Coventry, West Midlands.

Plate 18. Ewelme Hospital, Oxfordshire.

Plate 19. The Hospital of St. Cross, Winchester, Hampshire.

Plate 20. *Spence's Hospital, Craven, North Yorkshire.*

Plate 21. *Browne's Hospital, Stamford, Lincolnshire.*

Plate 22. Forde's Hospital, Coventry, West Midlands.

Chapter 5

The Dissolution of the Monasteries

By the middle of the 1530s there were of the order of eight hundred mediaeval hospitals, more or less evenly distributed throughout the whole of England; when the Reformation was finally completed, some thirty years later, only a handful remained and those that had survived had been re-founded on secular lines and rebuilt in the new domestic collegiate style.

To understand fully the effects of the English Reformation upon hospital and almshouse provision, it is necessary to begin in the early years of the reign of Henry VIII and trace it through the trauma of the late 1530s, through the reign of Henry's son Edward VI, and that of his elder daughter Mary, with its brief Counter Reformation, to the accession of Elizabeth I (1533-1603).

The true Reformation, as compared with Henry VIII's excuse for the rape of much of England's architectural heritage, had its origins on the Continent, more particularly in the Germany of Martin Luther (1483-1546). The latter was an Augustinian friar and professor of theology at the University of Wittenberg in Saxony. He was deeply concerned by what he saw as his own sinfulness for which he was convinced he could never obtain God's forgiveness, and from his readings of the Epistles of St. Paul he gradually grew to believe that man could be saved only by the grace of God and not by any actions of his own. Thus he formulated the Doctrine of Justification by Faith, a faith given by God to man in the redemption of the world by his son in his great sacrifice at Calvary.

This doctrine was not particularly earth-shattering; it had its origins in the teachings of St. Augustine. But it was anathema to most Christians in an age when the church held so much store by ceremony, particularly the Mass where the body and blood of Christ was offered as a sacrifice, the forgiveness of sins following confession, the remission of punishment incurred by the sinner through prayer to the saints and through the purchase of indulgences.

It was over the matter of indulgences that Luther's first clash with the ecclesiastical establishment occurred. Originally indulgences had originated as the commutation of penances stipulated by priests at confession; in effect the payment of a fine instead of the carrying out of the penance itself. But gradually this was extended far beyond the purpose for which indulgences were intended and became a payment not only to save a sinner in this world but also in Purgatory, that place in the after-life where the departed souls were tormented before being allowed into God's presence. In 1517 Archbishop Albrecht of Mainz obtained papal approval to sell indulgences in order to repay a loan he himself had raised to defray his personal expenses in becoming an archbishop. Half of the proceeds of the sale of these indulgences was to go towards the building of St Peter's in Rome, and they were offered not only to the living but also for their dead friends and relatives. The sales pitch used was "when the penny rattles in the box the soul leaps out of Purgatory".

Luther was highly critical of these practices, not only the sale of indulgences themselves but also of the very notion that forgiveness would ensue from penance. He maintained that penitence was the only antidote for sin and nailed his famous Ninety-five Theses on the subject to the door of Wittenberg Cathedral so that all scholars at the university could debate them.

This was the beginning of a long controversy with the established church, the culmination of which was Luther's excommunication by the Pope. He challenged the authority of the councils of the church and particularly the condemnation of the Bohemian reformer Hus (1369-1415) and the very infallibility of the Pope himself. He published several tracts which were highly critical of the church's power and in one addressed "to the nobility of the German Nation" he claimed that the state actually had authority over the church, a notion which was subsequently taken up by Henry VIII as justification for his break with Rome.

Perhaps his most controversial reform was the rejection of transubstantiation, the belief that during the Mass the wine and bread were actually turned into the body and blood of Christ. For this he substituted a belief originally attributed to Wycliffe (1320-84) called consubstantiation, the belief that the bread and wine were present with the body and blood, but not combined with them or replaced by them. In the tract published denouncing transubstantiation he also rejected confirmation, penance, ordination, holy unction and even marriage itself and claimed that only baptism and communion had been ordained by Christ. His greatest and most lasting work was the most constructive; the translation of the Bible from Latin into German.

The German princes accepted Luther's teachings enthusiastically, not so much out of religious zeal as for practical reasons. The church had dominated their lives for centuries, not only through the Pope but also through the office of the Holy Roman Emperor. They eagerly latched on to a concept which would remove the church's control and give them the autonomy which they had craved for so long. Thus safe from prosecution, Luther's views were echoed and vigorously supported by other sects with similar views; Anabaptists who rejected the baptism of infants, and the followers of Ulrich Zwingli (1484-1531), a Swiss reformer with similar ideas to Luther and John Calvin (1509-64), actually born a Frenchman but also active in Switzerland. Paradoxically, the basic groundwork upon which all these reforms were built emanated from England, from the New Learning or Humanism, that philosophical branch of the Renaissance which was pioneered by Colet, More and particularly Erasmus, whose new Latin translation of the Greek New Testament differed in many respects from the authorised version.

Thus the interchange of these new, sometimes heretical concepts strengthened Lutherism and Calvinism on the Continent and began to nibble away at the foundations of the Catholic church in England just at the time when Henry VIII was beginning his long dispute with the Pope. The combination of the two events was to prove to be catastrophic for the established church. Within thirty short years the changes that were wrought emancipated the common man's approach to religion, imposed a new responsibility on the Crown, directly and indirectly altered the local government of urban areas and of course had the most profound effect on the architectural and artistic heritage of the whole kingdom; almost overnight most of the great buildings were totally destroyed and almost all of the church's regalia, irreplaceable treasures, were melted down for bullion.

As alluded to above, the English Reformation had its origins in a secular rather than a religious dispute.

Following the untimely death of his older brother Arthur the Prince of Wales, Henry, at the age of twelve, became betrothed to his widow, Catherine of Aragon, six years his senior. His father, Henry VII, sought and obtained the dispensation of Pope Julius II, since then as now it was illegal to marry one's dead brother's wife. Six years later in 1509, the year of Henry's accession, Henry and Catherine were married. During the early years of their marriage the couple were happy and Henry showed his wife every courtesy and respect. But their happiness was marred by Catherine's inability to provide the king with a son. One boy had been born in 1511 but he died within two months and another, born two years later, died within hours of birth. The only child to survive was their daughter, Mary.

With the Wars of the Roses still fresh in the memory of many of his subjects, Henry was acutely aware of the threat to the peace of his realm that could ensue from the lack of a male heir; the House of York still had its survivors and supporters and nothing seemed more likely to provoke civil war than the succession of a female to the throne. The last woman to rule England had been Henry I's daughter Matilda in the twelfth century, whose accession was followed by years of bloody strife.

Henry was a devout Catholic, not only attending Mass with almost superstitious regularity, but also taking a keen interest in the theological debates of the day. His interest and depth of knowledge was not altogether surprising since before Arthur's death as second son, Henry seemed destined to become Archbishop of Canterbury rather than King.

As the years rolled by and no son and heir emerged, Henry became increasingly convinced that his bad luck was God's punishment for his marrying his brother's widow, for in the book of Leviticus was it not written: "Thou shall not uncover the nakedness of thy brother's wife", with a further threat that childlessness would result for those who broke the commandment. His disillusion became even more acute as Catherine lost her looks and strength with frequent and unrewarding pregnancies, and it was not surprising that he became susceptible to the charms of a nubile young girl with captivating eyes, Anne Boleyn.

Anne's refusal to grant Henry her charms outside the marriage bed, coupled with his increasing guilt concerning his marriage to Catherine, strengthened his resolved to seek an annulment to the marriage. Henry decided that the Pope's original decision to grant a dispensation for his betrothal to Catherine was erroneous and that as a consequence he was not legally married. Indeed he went as far as to instruct two archbishops, Wolsey and Warnham, to try him for incest. A verdict of guilty would, he argued, be endorsed by the Pope, particularly since doubts had already been expressed by theologians on Julian's dispensation and the marriage of Henry's sister Margaret of Scotland had been annulled on far less plausible grounds.

The two archbishops, Wolsey and Warnham, did not however respond with the alacrity which Henry expected. Indeed they prevaricated for months and took the advice of their fellow bishops, who for the most part declared that Henry and Catherine were legally married. In the end Henry decided to petition the Pope direct and to send a representative to Rome to ask if he could marry Anne without having to wait for a legal decision on the validity of his marriage to Catherine.

Wolsey strongly advised Henry against such a course of action and as a compromise arranged for the Legatine Court in London to consider the whole matter, although the final decision would remain with Pope Clement.

Contrary to Henry's expectation, Compeggio, the Papal Legate, began by trying to bring about a reconciliation between the king and the queen. When Henry proved to be intractable, Catherine was asked if she would set him free by entering a nunnery, but she refused. It was clear that the Church was not inclined to favour Henry's case, particularly since Catherine herself was opposed to the suit and the discovery that Julius, the Pope who had originally agreed to the betrothal, had anticipated Henry's objections in his original dispensation.

It was soon clear that an annulment was not to be forthcoming and Wolsey was blamed by Henry and Anne Boleyn who nursed an intense dislike of the Prelate. He was indicted for *praemunire*, that is allowing a court, the Legatine Court, to sit in England where only the king's writ was recognised, and was required to resign as Chancellor. He died soon afterwards and by doing so was thought to have cheated the hangman.

Wolsey was replaced by Sir Thomas More (1478-1535), a surprising choice since although he was at the time a firm friend of the king, he was a staunch Catholic and did not support him in his plans to marry Anne.

Meanwhile, two more of Henry's servants and supporters in his attempt to divorce Catherine informed him of a suggestion made by one of their Cambridge colleagues that he should ask the European Universities for their views on the legality of the marriage. Opinions were duly sought and Henry was delighted when such august centres of learning as Oxford, Cambridge, Paris, Bruges, Bologna and Padua all concurred that the marriage was illegal. To Henry's disgust however, Luther himself did not side with the king as expected. Instead, he argued that the ban imposed in Leviticus related to cases where the brother was still alive.

Nevertheless, the Cambridge scholar who had made the original suggestion to consult the universities was singled out for high office. He was Thomas Cranmer (1489-1556), who within a very short time was to be created Archbishop of Canterbury. Like many of his contemporaries, even he came to a sticky end.

The mood of the middle classes, particularly the intelligentsia, was becoming more and more anticlerical, or more correctly anti-Rome, as humanism began to permeate the fabric of scholarship and religion. Naturally enough the ground swell of change did not reach many people outside the centres of learning and London. Parishioners at local level had always relied upon their priest to instruct them; after all, most of them were unable to read the tracts and pamphlets which were being imported into the country from Lutheran Europe.

But this new Protestantism, allied with antagonism against Rome, began to have its effect when the new Parliament met in 1529. In the first session, the Commons introduced a series of bills to deal with a number of clerical abuses and to reduce the income which the clergy received, particularly those relating to probate and mortuary fees. Next, pluralism and non-residence were attacked by a bill which forbade clergy to take farmland beyond what was necessary for the support of their household, to keep a brewery or a tannery, or otherwise to trade for gain. These restrictions related only to the parish clergy, whose pluralities were ordained by the Pope. Of course, those approved by Henry himself, generally to his cronies, were acceptable.

The effect on the Pope was firstly to summon Henry to appear before the Rota, the supreme court in Rome, and secondly to issue a bull prohibiting anyone from speaking or writing against the validity of Henry's marriage with Catherine, or any court from attempting to pass judgement on it.

Henry retaliated by invoking the law of *praemunire* which declared that those who brought Papal bulls into England or receive them:

"which touched our lord the king, against him, his Crown and Royalty, or his realm, shall be put out of the king's protection, and their lands, tenements, goods and chattels forfeited to our lord the king, and that they be attached by their bodies and brought before the king and the Council".

Writs were issued against many clerics, particularly bishops for assisting Wolsey and for bribing him to prevent him from overriding their Episcopal authority. Before these cases were heard, Henry indicted the whole of the clerical estate accusing them all of *praemunire*, particularly of accepting Wolsey's legatine authority or of exercising their jurisdiction in the church courts. Convocation met in January 1531 and in order to placate Henry and to obtain his pardon, paid a fine of £10,000. Moreover, in addition to paying him money the clergy agreed to acknowledge Henry as their "Singular protector only and supreme lord....even supreme head" but with an important proviso, "so far as the law as Christ allows". This did not go quite so far as to replace the Pope's authority with that of the king. That was to be delayed for twelve months or so.

The year 1532 began by Convocation falling over itself to impose tighter control over the clergy, particularly ordinands who were expected to undertake at least six hours' Bible study each week. Parliament was not impressed, and commenced its session with a presentation to the king of a Supplication Against the Ordinaries. Some scholars think that this was a document drafted by Thomas Cromwell about three years earlier whilst still a member of the House of Commons. The Supplication demanded a single sovereignty and undivided allegiance, linking together control over church courts and Convocation. It attacked the power of the latter to make laws without consulting the laity; it attacked the church courts for prosecuting for trivial matters and for imposing unreasonably high fees, the sale of sacraments, the presentation of minors to benefices and the encouragement of idleness by the holding of an excessive number of holy days.

Henry welcomed the initiative taken by the Commons and demanded that Convocation should pass no new laws without his express approval.

He pointed out that the prelates' oaths to the Pope were "clean contrary to the oath they make to us so that they seem his subjects, not ours".

Convocation, realising that both king and Parliament were ranged against it, capitulated almost immediately and submitted to the king's demands. Sir Thomas More, seeing the writing on the wall, resigned his Chancellorship the next day.

Whilst the Commons were attacking Convocation, Henry encouraged the House of Lords to legislate against annates, those payments out of ecclesiastical income to the Holy See. The bill, The Conditional Restraints of Annates, described them as "great and inestimable sums of money daily conveyed out of this realm to the impoverishment of the same", and declared that payment was to cease. Henry was trying to blackmail the Pope into a favourable decision concerning the annulment of his marriage, although as time went on some members of both houses had reservations concerning his actions, the Commons because the wool trade with the Continent might suffer, and of course the bishops and abbots sitting in the House of Lords were opposed because of their allegiance to the Pope.

The Act when approved anticipated retaliation from Rome by declaring that should the Pope delay or deny bulls of consecration, bishops would be consecrated by English authority alone. Moreover, should excommunication ensue, the English people would "without any scruple of conscience" continue to receive the sacrament and attend church services without the Papal blessing.

Later on in the year 1532 Archbishop Warnham died. He had continued to support the papacy against Henry's actions, particularly the divorce, and was replaced by Thomas Cranmer, the scholar who a few years previously had suggested that Henry should consult the European Universities. He had risen to be Archdeacon of Taunton and Ambassador to the Imperial court. And he was married.

By early 1533 Anne Boleyn had succumbed to Henry's persuasion and was pregnant. On 25th January they were secretly married, so that the expected son would not be illegitimate. Cranmer, by this time properly installed as Archbishop with, surprisingly, the Pope's bull of Consecration, officiated, and by doing so formally put the seal on Henry's conduct, paving the way for the annulment which followed in the May of that year. Prior to that, though, a bill was introduced into Parliament, The Act in Restraint of Appeals, to prevent any attempt by Catherine to thwart the action by appealing to Rome. The annulment was proclaimed at a special court meeting at Dunstable following the passing of a resolution by a much depleted Convocation, that the Pope had no right to permit the marriage of Henry and Catherine. There then followed a decree proclaiming Henry's marriage with Anne to be valid and the queen was crowned. Henry, thinking that because Cranmer had been pronounced legate of the Apostolic See by Pope Clement, thought that the archbishops' verdict would be confirmed, but he was mistaken. Clement declared in June that Anne was not Henry's wife, and the king was excommunicated.

The Pope's action brought about a spate of legislation which, during 1534, tightened Henry's grip on the English church. The Act for the Submission of The Clergy endorsed the Commons' Supplication Against the Ordinaries of 1532 and imposed a fine or imprisonment at the king's pleasure upon all who acted contrary to its provisions. Appeals to Rome were forbidden; in their place were allowed appeals from the archbishop's court to commissioners in chancery. The Conditional Restraint of Annates was now made absolute by an act of that name, which also prevented Papal bulls being procured for the consecration of bishops and abbots, confirming the practice whereby the king chose his own bishops. Henceforth he would also have the right to select abbots, monastic chapters having to petition the crown under pain of *praemunire*.

Another act, the Dispensation Act, stopped all payment to Rome including Peter's Pence, and removed the Pope's authority concerning departures from Canon Law. Even at this late stage Henry hoped that his differences with Rome could be resolved, but on 23rd March 1534 Clement finally closed the royal case and formally pronounced Henry's first marriage to be valid.

By the time that Parliament assembled in November 1534, Henry had achieved all that he had set out to obtain; an annulment to his first marriage; a new wife; a new heir, and virtual control of all the church in England. All this was confirmed by the Act of Supremacy which declared:

"Albeit the King's Majesty justly and rightfully is and oweth to be supreme head of the Church of England, and so is recognized by the Clergy of this realm in their Convocation, yet nevertheless for corroboration and confirmation thereof, and for the increase of virtue in Christ's religion within this realm of England, and to repress and extirp all errors, heresies and other enormities and abuses heretofore used in the same, be enacted by the authority of this present Parliament that the King our Sovereign Lord, his heirs and successors, Kings of this realm shall be taken accepted and reputed the only Supreme Head in earth of the Church of England."

However, prior to the Act of Supremacy the Pope had exercised two kinds of power in the land, Potestas Jurisdictionis, administrative power, and Potestas Ordinis, the right to administer the sacraments, to excommunicate and to preach. Henry was no priest and as a consequence had none of the spiritual powers; only the administrative ones. The Church of England might have a new head but essentially it had changed very little. It remained for some considerable time at least a Catholic country in everything but name.

Henry's new powers were not accepted universally. All the clergy were required to swear an oath of allegiance and most did so, the bishops surrendering their Papal bulls, being re-appointed under royal letters patent. But two well-known personalities refused to take the oath. Bishop Fisher of Rochester and Sir Thomas More. Both were committed to the Tower pending the passing of an Act which made it possible to commit verbal treason, which would include "maliciously attempting to deprive the king, queen and their heirs of their dignity, title and name of their royal estates". Fisher admitted that he had said that the king could not possibly be the Supreme Head on earth of the Church of England and was beheaded at Tyburn in June 1535. Two weeks later Sir Thomas More followed him.

Once the church was under the direct control of the Crown the king began to tap its vast wealth. The Act in Conditional Restraint of Annates of 1533 and the Act in Absolute Restraint of Annates of 1534 had both prohibited the payment of fees to the Pope in Rome as an "intolerable burden". However, after the passing of the Act of Supremacy they were now made payable to the Crown. Consequently, upon entering a new living or church office, secular or monastic, the incumbent was required to make a payment to the Crown. Not only that, all clergy were to pay one tenth of their annual income to the king; moreover, he was not content to accept an assessment of 1292 as the Pope had been. He wanted the full up-to-date value, and to ensure that this was extracted in full he appointed as his Vicar General the son of a Putney blacksmith, who had risen to high office by his own genius for administration, Thomas Cromwell (1485-1540).

Cromwell's origins are somewhat obscure. He had some legal training and worked for a short while as a banker in Italy and the Netherlands, before becoming a member of Parliament in 1523. In the same year he entered the service of Cardinal Wolsey, where his future was foreshadowed somewhat when he was instrumental in suppressing twenty-nine religious houses in order to provide for the foundation of the cardinal's new colleges for the clergy at Ipswich and Oxford.

Upon Wolsey's fall, Cromwell made himself useful to the king by helping to transfer the Cardinal's forfeit see at Winchester, his Abbacy of St. Albans and his educational establishments to the royal treasury. Gradually his genius for administration assured his preferment, when in 1533 he was made the Chancellor of the Exchequer, and one year later Principal Secretary. His influence upon Henry in those early years was considerable. He was conversant with all current political thought, particularly that espoused by Machiavelli and Marseglio, whose Defensor Pacis asserted that temporal rulers were invested with the duty of reforming the church and denied the Pope's claim to pre-eminence among the bishops as the successor to St. Peter since, as he pointed out, Peter enjoyed no pre-eminence over the other apostles, and had never been to Rome anyway! Clearly, Cromwell's influence, particularly his views on the position of the Crown regarding the church, helped to spur Henry into the actions which he took. Furthermore, Cromwell's excessively authoritarian views turned the king's attention towards the increasingly decadent monastic system, and his avarice towards the immense wealth which was there for the taking. In order to assess the extent of this great wealth, Cromwell undertook a survey, the Valor Ecclesiasticus, sending commissioners throughout the length and breadth of the country .

By 1530 there were approximately 825 separate religious houses in England and Wales, five hundred odd monasteries, one hundred and thirty-six nunneries and the remainder friaries of the main three types, Franciscan, Dominican and Augustinian.

The Valor confirmed Cromwell's suspicions. Collectively, the total income of all houses was some £160,000 a year, worth perhaps £6.6 millions in to-day's money. The richest was, as might be expected, the Benedictine Abbey at Westminster, whilst at the other extreme, about ten percent were worth less than £20 per annum. Several houses were centres of pilgrimage and received regular incomes from visitors, although by far the most important source of wealth was land and the rents and tithes which accrued to it. Recent estimates claim that the clergy owned up to one sixth of the entire realm.

In view of this immense wealth belonging to a church which Henry had in fact taken over, an income some three times greater than that of the Crown itself, it was not altogether surprising that he should, with Cromwell's prodding, decide to expropriate some of it for his own use. Accordingly in 1536, by an Act passed by an enthusiastic and supportive Parliament, he dissolved the houses, with an income of less than £20 per annum. He confiscated such income as was available for internal administrative use and in preparation for defence against possible attack by critics of the church settlement.

The main reason for the closure of the smaller monasteries, other than Henry's wish to lay his hands on their wealth, was their laxity – their failure to perform their religious duties. Many abbots and abbesses forgot or ignored their vows of poverty, and in some cases those of chastity also. Over the years many visitors had found the religious enjoying a higher standard of living than their lay contemporaries. Abbots and priors lived liked princes, often exchanging their habits for fine vestments and jewellery with huge retinues of attendants. In many cases, even the smaller houses which were to be closed, had long neglected their religious duties and were merely places of abode for occupants and a source of free board and lodging. It is true to say that external influences often played their part, as stewards – often landed gentry with influence in high places – and founders and their descendants, extracted large payments in cash and kind, and by their actions and interference, diverted the religious from their duties.

Following the Act of Supremacy, visitations by officers of the Crown replaced those by the bishops. The Valor had assessed the wealth which the monasteries enjoyed, and the suppression of the smaller houses was just the prelude to wholesale closure. It is almost certain that Cromwell had this in mind from the beginning; only his Machiavellian cunning hid his true purpose from the country in general, as he adopted the softly, softly approach of gradual attrition.

Cromwell, as Vicar General, chose his new visitors carefully; two have come down in history as being particularly odious; Doctors Layton and Leigh, who were chiefly responsible for reports on the northern monasteries. It is generally accepted now that in their zeal to serve Cromwell and Henry they falsified and exaggerated their reports, painting a much bleaker picture than had been the case during previous visitations by the bishops. Indeed, it is difficult to take much of what they reported very seriously at all since they were reputed to have visited one hundred and twenty-eight monasteries and their dependent hospitals between December 1535 and February 1536, a rate of more than one every day!

Nevertheless, the reports were received by a receptive House of Commons and the Act to suppress the smaller houses was passed in the spring of 1535. Not all those put forward for dissolution were closed. Ninety-two were classed as part of their mother houses, because they were not regarded as separate entities in the administrative sense. The Gilbertines were also allowed to survive, probably because of the friendship of their prior, Robert Holgate, with Cromwell. Many more were allowed to continue for the time being at least, by their making generous gifts to the Vicar General. Altogether, only some two hundred and forty out of a total of six hundred and forty were closed.

Anticipating, perhaps, what was to follow in later years, Cromwell set up a new department of state to handle the affairs of the dissolved houses, the Court of Augmentations. The court's officials let off the land to adjoining owners and transported anything of value – gold, silver and lead – to London, whilst property of lesser value was auctioned off on the spot.

Generally, the dissolution went smoothly, although there were pockets of resistance, chiefly in the North and in Lincolnshire, which Cromwell was to use as his springboard for the dismantling of the rest of the monastic system. The Pilgrimage of Grace and the Lincolnshire Risings, generally thought to have been the result of ill-feeling against the persecution of the church, had more profound reasons. The rebellion which started in Lincolnshire and spread throughout Yorkshire however, was almost heaven sent for Cromwell's purposes. It took little effort to put it down, and when the heads of the larger houses which were involved were brought to justice, it was a simple matter to treat them as traitors and confiscate their property. Even those who were not directly involved at all, such as the prior of Furness in Lancashire, were accused and only found not guilty after they had surrendered their houses. This was helped considerably by the custom in the monastic system that the lands and properties of the house were vested in the prior alone, not the chapter. Consequently, he had to consult no-one when prevailed upon to give them up.

Not all the religious were badly treated though. Most were offered livings as lay priests or pensioned off, and most of the priors were offered bishoprics in the new cathedrals which were founded as part of Henry's reformation.

Late in 1537 the government decided upon the total dissolution of the monastic system. By December, four southern houses surrendered in similar circumstances to Furness and in February 1538 another royal commission set out to visit all the remaining houses, offering a prepared contract of surrender and rewards in the form of pensions and from the well-documented martyrdom of the London Charterhouse and a few other instances of the execution of the prior or abbot. The result of these sporadic persecutions was that all serious resistance was discouraged, and by March 1540 just two years later, the last surviving religious house in England and Wales, Waltham Abbey had surrendered.

Chapter 6

The Suppression
of the Chantries and the
Demise of the Hospitals

Henry VIII's administration was not only concerned with the dissolution of the monastic houses. The very core of Roman Catholicism had to be purged before the Church of England could reign supreme. And it was those rites and ceremonies perceived as superstitious practices to which the common people had long been accustomed and which formed the very nucleus of the old religion, particularly the notion of purgatory and fear of the hereafter, which had bound men to the church, and had been the source of so much of its revenue down the years.

This fear of purgatory and particularly the wish to avoid having to serve a long sentence there oneself before being admitted into heaven, as well as trying to prevent it happening to one's dear ones, gave rise to the doctrine of the remission of sins by prayer and intercession on behalf of the deceased by the saints.

The aristocracy could insure themselves against an uncomfortable after-life by the endowment of a chantry, a special chapel, or indeed just an altar within a church where prayers could be offered regularly for the souls of the departed benefactor and his family. Usually the prayers were accompanied by the burning of incense and candles with a light burning continually.

Ordinary people could not afford their own chantries; they could scarcely afford the benefit of a decent burial. So early on in medieval Europe they banded together to form fraternities or confraternities (the terms are synonymous) otherwise known as religious or parish guilds.

These guilds should not be confused with the craft or merchant guilds, although they did have some elements in common with them. The parish guilds were primarily burial clubs, the precursors of the Victorian friendly societies, providing money out of aggregated subscriptions for a decent interment plus regular prayers for the soul of the departed, either as part of an annual requiem mass or in the form of obits, special prayers offered on the anniversary of the death of the parishioner .

Every parish, however small, had its fraternity under the patronage of a particular saint or saints; the Trinity, Blessed Virgin Mary, Corpus Christi, St. John the Baptist, St. John the Evangelist or similar. Its principal function, as mentioned above, was to provide individual members with a good funeral, as solemn and well-attended a send-off as possible, together with regular prayers for his or her soul. But, like all social organisations, many guilds grew and in time were able to provide other facilities; they gave material help to younger members, they provided food and clothing and shelter in the form of hospitals and almshouses for their poor, sick and elderly brethren, as well as interest-free loans to widows and orphans and dowries for daughters. They often guaranteed help for members who fell on hard times because of fire, flood, theft or shipwreck, offering a kind of insurance service, and they acted as executors under the wills of deceased members.

At its most primitive level, the members would gather together on the patronal feast day to offer Masses for past and present brothers and sisters at the altar, or if the guild could afford one, at the chapel belonging to the fraternity. All living members had to contribute at least one 'Mass Penny' to help with the upkeep of the altar and the payment of the priest, but many guilds expected that members should bequeath a certain amount of their worldly goods to the fund – one shilling for every pound's worth of chattels, up to a maximum of forty shillings, in the case of St. Mary and the Holy Cross in Chesterfield, for instance – as well as special annual collections for alms.

As mentioned in previous chapters, many of the larger fraternities, such as those in Aylesbury, Banbury, Coventry, Chester, Chesterfield, Derby, Hull (St. Mary and Trinity), Maidstone, Newcastle, Taunton, Warwick and Worcester ran schools and almshouses for their members, and there is evidence that they provided much needed help for their less fortunate brethren right up to their dissolution after 1547. Many owned guildhalls or guild houses; we have already come across examples in Coventry and Wells, as well as tenements providing rent free accommodation for destitute members. Some guilds looked after bridges (there is a famous example in Wakefield), highways, sluices and sea walls; Birmingham's Holy Cross fraternity maintained a chiming clock and employed a midwife. Guild money built towers and spires as at Louth in Lincolnshire, and even whole churches as at Coventry and Bodmin.

These larger fraternities were dominated by the local town dignitaries; indeed upon the suppression of the guilds under Henry's son, Edward VI, many guild masters formed the nuclei of the town councils which were afterwards incorporated.

The larger guilds, centred upon the major towns, went far beyond the services provided by the local fraternities; indeed they provided services which could not by any stretch of the imagination be classed as charitable; banking, insurance and cultural and religious patronage. They were the major property owners, had splendid guildhalls and formidable rent rolls as a result of handsome endowments by wealthy benefactors, as well as regular subscriptions from thousands of members. They derived rents from lands, tenements, mills and barns and had memberships including dignitaries from England and surprisingly enough from the continent of Europe. Boston's St. Mary's guild had an income of over £900 in 1520; Coventry's Holy Trinity fraternity was probably the biggest single landlord in the city. Great institutions had aldermen, wardens, chamberlains to prepare the accounts, stewards to collect the annual subscriptions from far-flung members, almoners to administer their charitable works and cup-bearers, mace-bearers, choristers and organists, together with umpteen clergy. Coventry's Holy Trinity fraternity at Bablake, with its Bablake Hospital mentioned earlier, had thirteen full-time priests and the fine church of St. John.

With the dissolution of the monasteries completed by 1540, Henry and his close advisers were well on the way to cleansing the church of all popish influence. Of course much of the Church of England's litany was similar to that under true Catholicism, but by that time the grip on the common people by the clergy had been broken.

Following Cromwell's entrapment by Norfolk and Gardiner and subsequent execution, Henry married Norfolk's young niece Catherine Howard. The marriage did not last very long since the queen was convicted of adultery and beheaded two years later. The aspirations of some noblemen and bishops at least to halt the break with Rome, if not to reverse it, were shattered by several of Henry's next actions. Firstly, in July 1541 a royal proclamation was issued abolishing "the many superstitious and childish observations" on St. Nicholas' and Holy Innocents' Days when choristers were appointed boy bishops and preached to and blessed the congregations. Three months later it was ordered that all shrines should be dismantled and that the only lights which would be permitted to burn were those before the Blessed Sacrament.

The next Act in 1546 was to publish a revision of the Bishop's Book first published in 1537 as the "Institutions of a Christian Man". The new edition, as well as setting down who could and could not read the Bible, again repudiated "the pretended universal primacy of the Bishop of Rome" and defined the actions which would lead to Salvation as:

"inward spiritual work, motions and desires, as love and fear of God, godly meditations and thoughts, patience, humility and such like, not the superstitious works of men's own invention."

The people were warned not to "deck images gorgeously " and finally, with Cranmer's help and guidance he introduced the new English Litany which is to this day the basis of the Book of Common Prayer. In 1544, some four years after the surrender of the last monastic house to the Crown, Henry made his peace with the Emperor Charles V (1500-58) and joined him against England's long-standing enemy, France. As usual, the campaigns on the Continent were costly affairs and the king had to seek new ways of raising revenue, as by now he had spent virtually all the receipts from the closure of the monasteries. This time, the main source of finance was the chantries and fraternities, especially those with wealthy endowments and lavishly ornamented chapels. An Act of 1545 gave him the right to expropriate the relevant property, a privilege of which he availed himself immediately, although not in as widespread a manner as when he dissolved the monasteries.

At the suggestion of Cranmer and one or two other bishops, the opportunity was taken whilst drafting the Act to ban several long standing practices which were associated with Chantries and considered to be equally superstitious. They included bellringing on Halloween, the covering of images during Lent, kneeling to the Cross on Palm Sunday and creeping to the Cross on Good Friday. Moreover, having made his peace by this time with the king of France, Henry announced that the two kings would jointly:

"not only within half a year to have changed the Mass into a Communion, but also to have utterly extirpated and banished the Bishop of Rome and his usurped power out of both their realms and dominions."

However, as history shows, this certainly did not come about in France, and progress was slowed down in England somewhat by the death of Henry some six months later, in January 1547.

In preparing for his passing, Henry provided in his will for a Regency Council to conduct the affairs of state until his son and heir Edward, aged only nine years, should come of age. This council was headed by two prominent Protestants, Edward Seymour, the Earl of Hertford, and brother of Queen Jane, Prince Edward's mother, and therefore his uncle, and John Dudley, Viscount Lisle, the Lord Admiral. In the event, the council did not rule itself; Seymour took possession of the boy-king and persuaded the council to give him the Regency alone and the title of Lord Protector. He also took for himself the title of Duke of Somerset.

The new Lord Protector was greedy and ambitious, as well as being a devout Protestant, and like Cromwell before him saw the Church as a milch cow with wealth available not only to top up the coffers of state, but also to provide him with a personal fortune.

Originally the Act of 1545 for the dissolution of chantries, guilds and the like empowered the king to dissolve only such chantries which had been the victims of embezzlement or had been already wound up by private initiatives and, an important provision, its powers lapsed with the death of the king. However, to many founders and guildsmen, the writing was already on the wall, and their worst fears were realised when only eleven months after Henry's demise a new Bill was laid before Parliament which provided for the expropriation of all chantries, guilds including secular ones, fraternities, all surviving colleges of secular clergy, and the handing over to the Crown of all endowments for Masses, obits and prayers for the dead, together with all properties and regalia connected therewith. In the event secular guilds were omitted from the Act's provisions when it was made law, due to the outcry from the London livery companies who otherwise would have come within its ambit. Nevertheless, the measure was to be of far-reaching importance for parish life in the future, and during the next few years the changes were to be most traumatic with not only the guilds themselves attacked but also most of the furnishings, plate and other regalia of parish churches being declared superstitious and confiscated by an avaricious Lord Protector.

The preamble to the Chantries Act stated that superstitious errors and ignorance of salvation through the death of Christ had been caused "by devising and phantasying vain opinions of purgatory and Masses satisfactory to be done for them which be departed". These false beliefs had been chiefly maintained by the abuse of chantries, but now the superstitious institutions could be put to good and godly uses as in the erection of grammar schools "to the education of youth in virtue", the further augmenting of the universities and better provision for the poor and needy. In the event, very few new schools and almshouses were founded using sequestered funds; the needs of the latest war with France and Somerset's private coffers saw to that.

It has been estimated that some two thousand, three hundred and seventy-five chantries and chapels were involved, ninety colleges of secular priests and significantly from the present study's point of view, one hundred and ten hospitals. The great majority of these hospitals actually survived, although in most cases this was due to the action of the municipalities and sometimes individuals who having bought them from the Crown (or more properly paid a fine for their retention), administered them thereafter on a municipal basis. A good example of this was the hospital attached to the Corpus Christi Guild in Poole, Dorset. This hospital was founded in the reign of Henry V, appropriated by the Crown in 1547 and bought back by the burgesses of Poole in 1550. The buildings, now converted to almshouses, are still there, within twenty-five yards of the parish church in the old town. Bablake in Coventry has already been described in some detail. Actually, the burgesses of Coventry objected to the bill as drafted and were placated by Somerset with the promise that "if they desisted from speaking or labouring further against the said article" they would be given back their guild lands once the Act was passed. The objections were withdrawn but the townsmen soon found that they had been duped; much of the property of the Holy Trinity Guild, Bablake was indeed returned to them – at a cost of £1,300 down and £90 per annum thereafter.

One rather crafty way of preventing the takeover by the Crown was the revival of an old custom " feoffment to use," whereby the legal title to the property in question – in this case land held by guilds and fraternities – was transferred to a sympathetic purchaser who leased back the property to the town so that the use could continue. This ruse had been used by some monasteries in 1536 to avert the takeover of their lands, but they had been thwarted because they proposed to continue with the religious use. The Crown could not make that allegation in the case of the guilds, because the properties involved were to be used for charitable rather than religious uses. A good example of this practice was that used by the Fraternity of the Holy Trinity in St. Botolph's Without, Aldersgate, in London, who obtained royal permission to transfer their hospital and guildhall to William Harvey, a herald and one of their members. Within two days the property was leased back to the Corporation, although of course it was prevented from using it for superstitious uses.

During the 1530s London lost many of its hospitals. York lost thirteen of its original twenty-two including St. Leonard's. Whilst the Edwardian Act did not relate specifically to hospitals, many were lost along with the dissolved guilds. For example, Fyfield in Berkshire and Alkmonton in Derbyshire lost the almshouses attached to their fraternities because, being in rural areas, no one with any influence was available to help. Some towns did get their almshouses back, but only after Edward had been dead for many years. Brutan in Somerset got its back after twenty years; Abingdon's guild hospital was closed in 1548 and restored five years later as Christ's Hospital; St. John's, Leicester, housing six old men, was also dissolved in 1548 and restored in 1589, during Elizabeth I's reign; Lambourn in Berkshire lost both its chantry school and almshouses. It had to wait forty years for its almshouses to be restored and a decade to recover any of its hospitals, despite the efforts of the great livery company.

Protector Somerset's rule ended in 1549, when, after trying to rouse the common people to support him in his feud with the conservative faction in the Council, he was sent to the Tower and later, after more intrigue, to the block. Warwick, one of the original Regency council members nominated by Henry VIII, replaced Somerset as Lord Protector and was to prove to be even more of a tyrant than his predecessor. He lost little time in creating himself Duke of Northumberland and, like Somerset, squeezed the chantries and fraternities to the benefit of the public purse and his own. But his influence was also relatively short-lived; Edward died in early 1553 and with his death the Reformation in England came to a halt for a brief period.

Mary, Edward's half sister, the daughter of Catherine of Aragon, became queen following Northumberland's abortive attempt to place his daughter-in-law, the unfortunate Lady Jane Grey, on the throne. She promptly turned the clock back and re-introduced Roman Catholicism, complete with a tyranny which rivalled the Spanish Inquisition.

Although Mary's short reign was terrifying in many respects – over eight hundred Protestant zealots were burned at the stake – it had its compensations, especially as regards the fraternities' lands. Abingdon received back much of the property of the Holy Cross Fraternity. Boston, Bridgwater, Clitheroe, Mansfield, Sheffield and Walsall all had lands, particularly hospitals and almshouses restored; Basingstoke had all its Holy Cross Fraternity lands returned; Derby had property worth £77 given back belonging originally to its Abbey and Holy Trinity Guild. The townsmen who took over the responsibilities of the guilds had in the process become de facto corporations and lost no time in petitioning the Crown for Charters of Incorporation. In all thirty-five such towns were incorporated during Mary's reign.

Mary died in 1558 and with the advent of her half-sister Elizabeth to the throne, the Protestant religion was restored once more, never again to be usurped. From our study's point of view, the main effect was that mediaeval hospitals with their administration by monks and guildsmen disappeared for ever, and the provision and endowment of the almshouses which replaced them was left to others.

Chapter 7

The Elizabethan Period

The Elizabethan period marked the transition from mediaeval to modern times. The Renaissance was in full swing on the Continent, although it would be some years before its impact would be felt in England. But the revolution in thought, particularly the Humanist theories which were expounded by Erasmus and Calvin, reverberated throughout the land and was espoused by many of the Marian exiles who had been exposed to these theories constantly during their sojourn in Germany and the Low Countries.

The queen herself, whilst almost certainly sympathetic to many of the new ideas, at first was prudent enough to tread the middle path, certainly during the early years of her reign, until policies both secular and religious had been developed, and a council of ministers suited to her style of government properly recruited.

England, whilst still a predominantly rural country, enjoyed an increasingly improving standard of living for the rank and file with a much more comfortable existence than their counterparts across the Channel. Industry was developing and internal trade increasing. Although full-time wage earners were in the minority during the majority of the reign, most people had some work, but it was difficult for unskilled workers to earn more than a bare subsistence.

A series of disastrous harvests devastated the whole of Europe during the 1590s, encouraging Elizabeth and her ministers to introduce legislation to influence social conditions, particularly for the relief of poverty and the control of the economy. During the reigns of earlier Tudor monarchs, poor relief had been left to the parishes to raise and distribute. The Act of 1536 limited the receipt of alms to friars, shipwrecked mariners, the lame and the blind, although all poor people were permitted to continue to solicit "broken meats and refuse (waste) drink". Parish funds were established as obligatory "by gathering of such charitable and voluntary alms every Sunday, Holy Days and other Festivals".

Parishes were threatened corporately with fines of 20 shillings per month for default. Non-resident clergy with incomes of less than £20 had to contribute at least a fortieth of their income in alms, and churchwardens saw to it that they did. The Vagabond Act of 1547 invited parishes to erect houses for the accommodation of the disabled poor, and a similar act of 1552 set up parish registers of the poor, and authorised the parish officers to report to the bishop anyone who declined to contribute to the poor box. The Act of 1563 authorised bishops to bind over recalcitrants in the sum of £10 to appear before a Justice of the Peace, whose duty it was to assess the culprits and make them pay a weekly instalment under threat of imprisonment. Since it was feared that the plague, still endemic in Europe, was spread by beggars, a system of licensing them was introduced, together with measures to confine them to their homes.

Lincoln opened a poor relief fund in 1550 to which aldermen and other citizens contributed. London, Norwich, Exeter, Cambridge and

Ipswich followed suit making poor contributions compulsory for all households of ability. In 1572 a Poor Rate was introduced with collectors and local overseers of the poor appointed by Justices of the Peace.

By 1580 poverty was much more widespread, particularly among wounded soldiers and sailors, and begging was rife. Unlicensed beggars over the age of 14 were whipped and branded; those under 14 were whipped and put out to apprenticeships.

Between the years 1594 and 1597 the price of grain doubled and many people died of starvation. The statutes of 1597 and 1691 established a system of parochial poor relief which lasted until 1834. Also, between 1570 and 1600 several charity hospitals in the modern sense of the word and over one hundred sets of almshouses were established to nurse the sick. The provision of such almshouses was pursued throughout Elizabeth's reign and continues up to the present-day.

Apart from the general need to relieve poverty, three elements contributed directly or indirectly to the foundation of these new almshouses; the Elizabethan Settlement, the rise of the merchant classes and the rise of the gentry.

When Elizabeth ascended the throne in 1558, the country was at war simultaneously with Scotland and France. The religious divisions which had beset it since her father's death had weakened authority and created deep divisions in society. The aristocracy had been decimated during almost a century of strife. Norfolk was the only duke in England, there was no Archbishop of Canterbury and nine of the Episcopal sees were vacant. What was needed was a new religious settlement which would reach out to both factions, Catholic and Protestant alike and impose some semblance of harmony in religious affairs.

In choosing new members of her Council, the queen retained the moderate elements of the previously predominantly Catholic faction, and supplemented them with Protestants. A Supremacy Bill had a rough passage through Parliament and was finally approved only when Elizabeth declared herself the Supreme Governor rather than the Head of the Church of England as her father had been. She appointed no Vicar General as Henry had appointed Cromwell, but instead exercised her jurisdiction over the Church through a Court of High Commission staffed by lay members and lawyers, as well as clerics. On the delicate question of uniformity, the Book of Common Prayer followed the example set in the second book of Edward VI, but at the crucial points changes were introduced to widen the numbers of those who could join in Communion in the parish churches. Words were chosen that would allow both conscientious Catholics and Protestants to participate in the service.

The clergy were enjoined to use the book on pain of imprisonment, and the laity, for its part, had to attend church every Sunday, and when absent had either to give a satisfactory explanation to the church warden or pay a fine of one shilling. Most important, the rules against the clergy marrying were relaxed. As a result, many hundreds of young parsons availed themselves of this opportunity and during subsequent decades their offspring formed the backbone of middle-class society.

The Statute of Artificers (or Statute of Apprentices) of 1563 was the most comprehensive enactment to control economic life which had yet been undertaken by any European government. It co-ordinated the law on employment in towns and the availability of agricultural labourers, its aim being to stabilise the existing class structure and with it the location of industry and the transfer of labour from one place to another. Although it was restrictive on the movement of labour, it was specific in its encouragement of trade; the restrictions in fact related only to existing industries. New industries which were beginning to appear were not hampered by limitations on apprenticeships, labour contracts or locality.

The progress of industrialisation was growing apace. In the early years of the reign, England was as dependent on the import of foreign, manufactured goods as she had been under previous monarchs. With the religious tolerance shown towards both Catholics and Protestants, persecuted artisans from all over the Continent arrived bringing with them the secrets of their trades. Textile workers from the Low Countries settled in the Midlands and Suffolk, manufacturing much lighter and finer materials than the old English cloths. They were followed by the French Huguenots and later German metallurgists who were persuaded to come to England to help to exploit the indigenous metals; tin, copper, iron and lead.

As tradesmen imparted their skills, so too did entrepreneurs and financiers. Later on, markets were needed for the surplus manufactured goods and a new breed of businessman, the merchant adventurer emerged. The search for new markets also spawned a breed of explorer/privateer. Sir Walter Raleigh founded the first, if short-lived English colony in America in 1585, and in 1600 the East India Company was incorporated which was destined to become the greatest economic organisation in England for over two centuries. Sir Francis Drake circumnavigated the world; Sir Humphrey Gilbert, more soldier than navigator, looked for the North West Passage to the Indies and discovered Newfoundland, and Sir John Hawkins of Plymouth carried slaves from the west coast of Africa to Spanish America.

In the very early days, the military expeditions against France and Scotland were expensive and were paid for partly by selling Crown lands and partly by borrowing in Antwerp. However, as time went by, trade improved out of all proportion and by 1574 Elizabeth's ministers had not only balanced the books but also accumulated substantial reserves. Throughout the rest of the reign, English finances were far more stable than those of either France or Spain, which gave England substantial advantages in the military and particularly the naval arenas.

As trade grew, so did the merchant classes, mainly in the mercantile centres of Bristol, Norwich and London. All classes of any standing were engaged in what was a national effort at social betterment. The nobility continued as they had done in the past to build dwellings for their retainers at their gates or in their towns. Lord Burleigh built almshouses in his home town of Stamford, Bess of Hardwick built a similar group at Derby and Lord Northampton, Trinity House, Greenwich. The gentry were more concerned with direct poor relief and in their wills made bequests for outright relief, whether as doles or as endowments. The merchants banded together into City companies just as the medieval guildsmen had done before them, and as their combined wealth grew, an increasing percentage of it was devoted to philanthropy. This corporate giving benefited both their decayed company members and the general public.

In this endeavour, London out-performed the rest of the country by an astonishing amount. Over one third of all charitable giving over the whole country between 1480 and 1660 derived from the capital, although surprisingly enough at no time during this period did London's population amount to much more than five percent of that of the whole realm. Skinners, leather-sellers, drapers, haberdashers all made generous provision for the poor, establishing almshouses, hospitals and schools, both inside the City and its environs and in the innumerable towns and villages from which their members had originally come.

One or two individual merchants stood out for their remarkable acts of generosity. Thomas Sutton, born and brought up in Lincolnshire, became the richest commoner in the land and gave the whole of his fortune to charity – some £130,000 – which by today's standards would equate to some £8 million. His most famous act was the purchase of the London Charterhouse, centre of the monastic resistance to Henry VIII, which had until then been owned by the Duke of Norfolk who had gone to the block in 1572. There, Sutton founded a famous public school with a hospital alongside for impoverished gentlemen, merchants, soldiers and royal servants. The school was relocated in 1872 to Godalming where space could be provided for expansion, but the almshouse is still there, accommodating forty or so pensioners, off Clerkenwell Road in the heart of London (Figure 33 and Plate 23).

Although by far the most generous of the Elizabethan philanthropists, Sutton was by no means the only one. Sir Martin Bowes, a Yorkshireman who made his fortune as a goldsmith, left a large bequest, one half for poor relief, one half for charitable purposes, and Sir Thomas Owe, a rich merchant tailor left a similar bequest. Sir James Lancaster was another who left all his money to charity, the greater part of it to the Skinners' Company of which he was a member. Most of the bequest was for the training of apprentices and for the dowries of young maids.

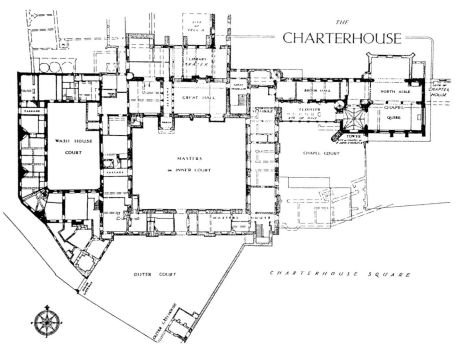

Fig 33. Plan of The Charterhouse, London.

The almshouses of the City companies were spread throughout Greater London as well as those provided by the parishes themselves. Within a stone's throw of Bishopsgate and Broad Street there were the almshouses of the Parish Clerks, those of the leather-sellers, the tailors, the linen-armourers as well as several groups built by individual benefactors.

Bristol was second only to London in philanthropic works, although it had a population of only 17,000. It was led by a merchant class "of great vitality, boldness and magnitude", making the most of opportunities after the Dissolution, buying ex-monastic properties for £1790, to which the parishes contributed £500 from the sale of church plate. The merchants were principally concerned with poor relief schemes for the unemployed and the founding of grammar schools. Robert Thorne left over £6000 for the founding of a school and for poor relief. Sir John Gresham left £2000 and even Henry VIII gave his doctor George Owen a parcel of land originally owned by the Order of St. John of Jerusalem, which was used for the support of ten almsmen, and William Chester purchased Black Friars which was also turned into almshouses. The merchant venturers established their own almshouses for aged seamen with endowments which produced £100 a year by 1600.

But perhaps the most significant social change in seventeenth century England was the rise of the gentry. This was brought about for several reasons. Firstly, as mentioned already, the decision to allow the clergy to marry in due course produced a group which although somewhat impoverished compared to the aristocracy, was well-educated and provided the raw material for country doctors, lawyers, schoolmasters and further clergy. Secondly, with the availability of ex-monastic lands, the nouveaux riches from the mercantile centres were able to purchase estates and establish themselves as country gentlemen. All towns, however small, exerted a tremendous influence on the surrounding countryside and, with the establishment of country estates, the new gentry in turn began to exert an influence on the towns. In mediaeval times, members of the House of Commons were returned by the townsfolk; they were truly representative of the townspeople. The House of Lords was as today staffed by the aristocracy. But with the rise of the landed gentry, townsmen were ousted from the borough seats to which, until the Reformation, they alone were entitled. To take the county of Wiltshire as an example, by 1584 only Salisbury returned two residents in accordance with statute; three other boroughs returned only one, a total of only five out of thirty four for the whole county. From 1559, Malmesbury only once returned a clothier, all its other members belonging to the gentry. Other cloth towns followed suit. Until then, townsmen in the House of Commons were concerned only with the narrow parochial view; with the introduction of the gentry, members of parliament were able to take a wider view of affairs as well as being better able to afford the expenses of sitting. With the mounting pressure by the gentry for parliamentary seats, many boroughs were incorporated to accommodate them, such as mere villages like Mitchell and Bosinney in Cornwall for which Sir Francis Drake sat. In 1584, of the 460 members of parliament, some 240 were country gentlemen.

Several important foundations date from this period. Perhaps the most important is Lord Leycester's (sic) Hospital at Warwick, founded by the queen's favourite, Robert Dudley in 1571 as a refuge for retired soldiers, once more using as a nucleus buildings previously occupied by religious guilds; the Guild of St. George, the Holy Trinity Guild and the Guild of St. Mary the Virgin. These buildings form surely the most picturesque group of almshouses in the country. Steeply roofed with shingles, timber framed and leaning rather drunkenly in places, and loosely arranged around a cobbled courtyard, the hospital is entered through an archway, itself surmounted by Dudley's crest, a bear and ragged staff. The buildings are still used for the same purposes today, housing eight retired servicemen, who on ceremonial occasions wear a mediaeval cap and gown, the uniform provided for them as part of the bequest of their founder over four hundred years ago. Figure 34 shows the plan of the hospital and its environs today, and Plate 24 shows a view of the hospital quadrangle and the covered access to the upper floors.

The Poor Travellers' Rest, a small almshouse founded in 1579 stands in Rochester High Street, immortalised by Charles Dickens in one of the Christmas numbers of "Household Words" in a short article "Seven Poor Travellers". It is interesting because it is an accurate account of life in this particular almshouse, albeit in Victorian times. He described it thus:

"I found it to be a white house, of a staid and venerable air, with a quaint old door, a choice little long low lattice window, and a roof of three gables.

"Howbeit, I kept my thoughts to myself, and accompanied the presence (the matron) to the little galleries at the back. I found them on a tiny scale, like the galleries in old inn yards; and they were very clean. While I was looking at them the matron gave me to understand that the prescribed number of Poor Travellers were forthcoming every night from year's end to year's end; and that the beds were always occupied. My question upon this and her replies brought us back to the Board Room so

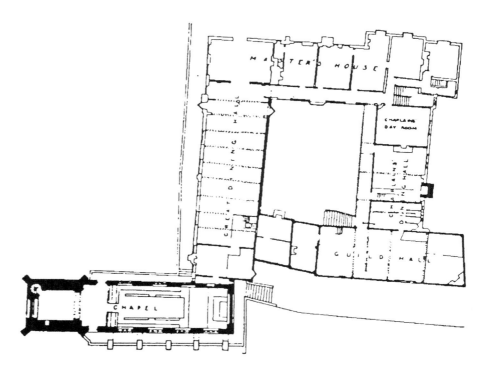

Fig 34. Plan of Lord Leycester's Hospital, Warwick, Warwickshire.

essential to the dignity of `the gentlemen' where she showed me the printed accounts of the charity hanging up by the window. From them I gathered that the greater part of the property bequeathed by the Worshipful Master Richard Watts for the maintenance of its foundation was, at the time of his death, mere marshland; but that, in course of time, it had been reclaimed and built upon, and was very considerably increased in value. I found too, that about a thirtieth part of the annual revenue was now expended on the purposes commemorated in the inscription over the door; the rest being handsomely laid out in Chancery, law expenses, collectorships, receiverships, poundage, and other appendages of management, highly complimentary to the importance of the Six Poor Travellers. In short, I made the not entirely new discovery that it may be said of an establishment like this, in dear old England, as of the fat oyster in the American story, that it takes a good many men to swallow it whole."

The inscription over the door, referred to above reads as follows:

RICHARD WATTS ESQ.
BY HIS WILL DATED 22 AUG 1579
FOUNDED THIS CHARITY
FOR SIX POOR TRAVELLERS
WHO NOT BEING ROGUES OR
PROCTORS
MAY RECEIVE GRATIS, FOR ONE
NIGHT
LODGING, ENTERTAINMENT,
AND FOUR PENCE EACH
IN TESTAMENT OF HIS
MUNIFICENCE
IN HONOUR OF HIS
MEMORY AND INDUCEMENT TO
HIS EXAMPLE
NATHL. HOOD, ESQ., THE PRESENT
MAYOR,
HAS CAUSED THIS STONE
GRATEFULLY TO BE RENEWED
AND INSCRIBED
A.D. 1771

Jesus Hospital, Rothwell, in Northamptonshire (Plate 25) was founded in 1591 by a local schoolmaster, Owen Ragdale, asking in return for the endowment that the inmates would have:

"special care and regard that his tomb in Rothwell church and the epitaphs, superscriptions, walls, pavements and other things therewith annexed, should be kept whole, safe, bright and clean."

The buildings, housing originally some thirty men, enclose a small quadrangular court, entered through a sturdy gateway.

Waldron's Almshouses, Tiverton, Devon (Plate 26) were also built in 1579, towards the close of the Elizabethan reign. Situated in Wellbrook Street, this picturesque set of almshouses was erected by John Waldron, a wealthy merchant, for the support of eight aged poor men who received two shillings each per week, eight shillings yearly for milk and twelve and sixpence on New Year's Day. The building has a little open gallery or arcade along the front and is festooned with plaques and shields, all making reference to the founder and his family. Unfortunately Waldron did not live to see the building's completion, as recorded on one of the inscriptions:

"John Waldron and Richard, his wife, builded this house in the tyme of his life, at such a tyme as the walls were fourteyne foot hye, he departed this worlde, even the eightynth of July (1579)."

John Whitgift, Elizabeth's Archbishop of Canterbury in her later years, founded in 1596 in Croydon what is in architectural terms perhaps the most typically "Elizabethan" group of almshouses in the country. The charity, dedicated to the "The Holy Trinity and the poor brethren and poor sisters of Croydon" was completed during the archbishop's lifetime, in order that he should not be a "cause of their damnation" to his executors. The building, quadrangular in plan, is of red brick, access to the courtyard being through an archway, over which are the arms of the founder and the See of Canterbury, with an archbishop's mitre and a motto:

"Qui dat pauperi non indigebat" (he who giveth to the poor shall not want).

The hospital provides accommodation for forty almsmen, together with a refectory, chapel and governor's lodgings, with rooms above where Whitgift himself stayed when visiting . The plan of the hospital is shown in Figure 35.

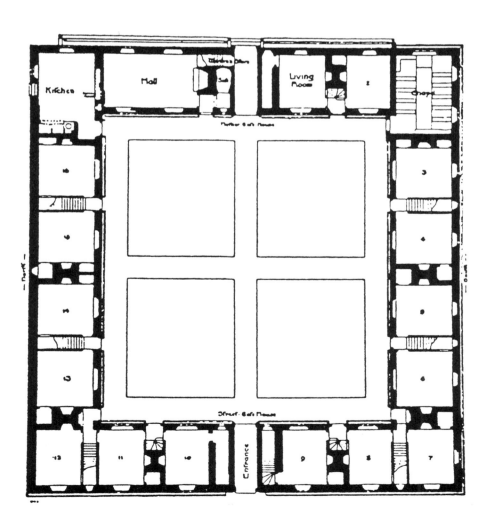

Fig 35. Plan of Whitgift's Hospital, Croydon, London.

Cobham College, Kent, was originally founded in 1362 for six chantry priests, but was refounded and rebuilt in 1598 for twenty almsfolk by William Brooke, Lord Cobham. Stone-built, around the usual quadrangle, the almshouse is situated close to the parish church and, as well as the accommodation for the old folk, had a hall and rooms for the warden and sub-warden. The plan of the college is shown in Figure 36, and a view of the courtyard in Plate 27.

Beamsley Hospital, that quaint circular shaped group of almshouses near Skipton, founded in 1593 by Ann Clifford, has already been referred to in an earlier chapter. Not many miles away, at Kirkthorpe near Wakefield, there exists another group, Frieston Hospital, very similar in concept to Beamsley but built to a square plan this time instead of circular, although many of its features lead one to believe that the same builder carried out the construction of both. Frieston Hospital was built in 1595, two years later than Beamsley, for John Frieston, the benefactor of Normanton Grammar School, who by a trust deed dated September 1592 conveyed:

"to the Master and Fellows of University College, Oxford and certain trustees and their heirs all his lands belonging to the Trinities in Pontefract upon confidence that the yearly rent and profits should go to the uses of the schoolmaster of his free school in Normanton and the poor people in his intended almshouse at Kirkthorpe."

The trust deed went on to direct that from the lands entrusted to the college:

"the sum of £20.16s. should yearly be paid towards the charitable relief and maintenance of seven poor, aged, and impotent men which shall

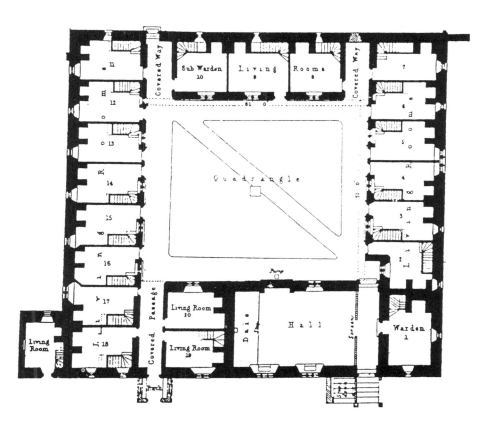

Fig 36. Plan of Cobham College, Kent.

be called Brethren and one poor aged and honest Matron which should be called a Sister, all of which persons should continue unmarried for ever and to whom there should weekly be allowed and paid upon the Saturday in the forenoon 12 pence to every one of the said eight poor and impotent aged persons for and towards their several relief and maintenance."

The seven men were housed in the hospital itself, a stone building with a central communal hall, in place of the central chapel at Beamsley, with seven small living rooms opening off it on three sides. The sister, who was employed principally as a laundress, was provided with a cottage on adjoining land. Another similarity to Beamsley is the turret or roof-light which provided daylight from above into the central hall. In the case of Beamsley it is circular; in the case of Frieston, it is rectilinear, the actual windows being in four dormers, one on each side. The plan of Frieston Hospital is shown in Figure 37 and a general photographic view in Plate 28. The almshouse was occupied until 1947 when it was closed and new dwellings provided nearby. The hospital building was sold and has since been converted into a private dwelling.

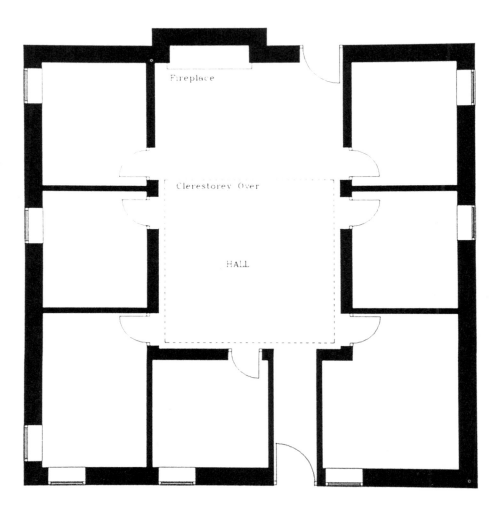

Fig 37. Plan of Frieston's Hospital, Wakefield, West Yorkshire.

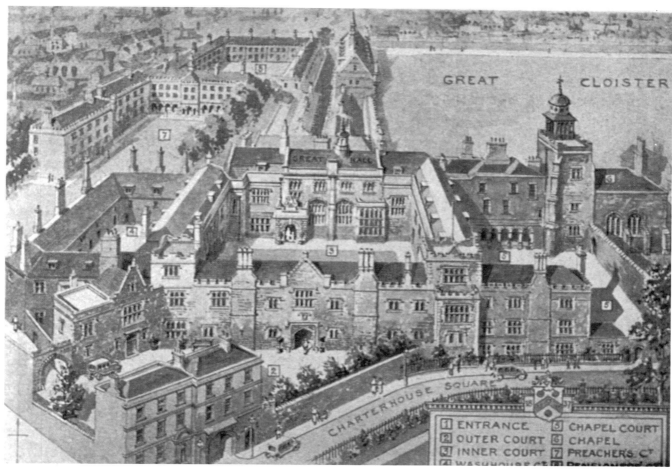

GREAT CLOISTER

GREAT HALL

CHARTERHOUSE SQUARE

1 ENTRANCE	5 CHAPEL COURT
2 OUTER COURT	6 CHAPEL
3 INNER COURT	7 PREACHERS. Ct

Plate 23. The Charterhouse, London.

Plate 24. Lord Leycester's Hospital, Warwick, Warwickshire.

Plate 25. Jesus Hospital, Rothwell, Northants.

Plate 26. Waldron's Almshouses, Tiverton, Devon.

Plate 27. Cobham College, Kent.

Plate 28. Frieston's Hospital, Wakefield, West Yorkshire.

Chapter 8

The Stuart Period

If the Elizabethan age marked England's transition from a mediaeval to a modern state, the period during which the Stuarts reigned, 1603 until 1714 marked the country's transformation from a minor European kingdom into the most important nation on earth, both militarily and economically. At the beginning of the period, the king, James I, ruled by divine right; at the end, George I owed his throne to an act of Parliament. James expected to "live on his own", financing government from his own personal resources, Crown lands, feudal dues and customs levies. By 1714, Queen Anne received a stipend and the control of the country's finances was vested in parliament.

In 1603 England was a second-rate power with no territories overseas other than Dunkirk; in 1714 she held a large empire in America, Africa, India and the Far East. The basic reason for this expansion of empire was the need to trade, to find an outlet for the products of the burgeoning economy brought about by the exploitation of the country's mineral resources, and the invention of machinery to mass produce items of clothing, particularly broadcloth, metal and pottery. Many of the great trading companies were formed specifically for this purpose; the East India Company, the Russia Company, the Merchant Adventurers' Company. In 1607 the East India Company made a profit of 500 per cent; in 1611 and 1612 the Russia Company paid a dividend of ninety per cent. Membership of these largely speculative organisations was restricted to a narrow circle. The entrance fee to the East India Company was £50, that for the Merchant Adventurers £200, enormous amounts by the standards of the day.

During this period, earthenware and glass replaced wood and pewter at table. Calico, linen and silk replaced leather for clothing, and the modern male attire of coat, waistcoat and breeches was introduced.

The Englishman's diet too was transformed; root crops were introduced, both as foods in themselves and as a means of keeping cattle alive during the winter. Potatoes, tea, coffee, and chocolate all were imported although only the former proved capable of being grown here. Agriculture was transformed by the Enclosure movement and by the invention of machinery. As a result, output rose astronomically, creating great wealth for the landowners, although conversely it created hardship for the peasants and copy-holders who were dispossessed.

The period was divided into four distinct phases; the rule of James I and Charles I, culminating in the Civil War (1603-1640), the Commonwealth (1640-1660), the Restoration (1660-1688) – embracing the reigns of Charles II and James II – and the Glorious Revolution (1688-1714), the reigns of William and Mary, William III and Queen Anne.

James VI of Scotland succeeded Elizabeth as James I of England (1566-1625); his son Charles succeeded him as Charles I (1600-49). Their reigns were marked by periods of chronic inflation. The price of wheat rose six times and the general price level four or five times. The overwhelming majority of the population lived by agriculture and the ruling classes on the rack rents derived from their tenantry. During the early period up to 1640 however, improvements were made, not only in securing a higher yield by the use of manures derived from beasts being kept over the winter, but by improvements in management, careful attention to book-keeping and keeping an eye on the markets.

"To improve land with profit", as Adam Smith was to say, "like all other commercial projects requires an exact attention to small savings and small gains of which a man born to great fortune, even though naturally frugal is seldom capable. The situation of such a person naturally disposes him to attend rather to ornament....than to profit."

Two phenomena assisted this agricultural transformation; the propensity of the king to dispose of Crown lands to provide money for his various extravagances – this enabled new and larger estates to be created as they were after the dissolution of the monasteries – and the enclosure of the open fields which since Norman times had been held from the Lord of the Manor by copy-holders in return for feudal payments of service or cash.

Enclosure had been going on since before Elizabeth, and indeed by 1600 the great age of enclosure for sheep farming was over. But under the new initiatives, the scattered strips in open fields were consolidated and hedged about to keep out people and cattle. They were experimented upon by the rotation of crops, the switching of arable to pasture and back again. Despite repeated government measures to prevent it, enclosure increased relentlessly during the seventeenth century with the inevitable movement of population from rural to urban areas. Moreover, with marginally longer life expectancy generally, and the increasing birthrate, the population was growing. This provided a further stimulus to increase agricultural output, if only to feed the increasing numbers. The emergence of industry, albeit in an embryo state, encouraged the development of areas with little or no reliance on agriculture; for the first time there were whole sectors of society which relied totally upon their ability to work, and thereby earn a wage to purchase food.

England was therefore relatively over-populated; that is to say the population was greater than the economy could support, and poverty was rife. Attempts were made to establish workhouses in which the poor could be set to work, although as in previous centuries there was a careful distinction drawn between the "deserving poor" and "sturdy rogues" who were deemed to be shirkers.

The increases in wealth which were brought about by the improvements in agricultural methods and industrial expansion were not shared by the labouring classes. Bad harvests were relatively frequent, as were famine and pestilence. This, together with taxation, both civil and ecclesiastical, fell most heavily on the poor. The average life expectancy, about thirty-five years, although increasing, was much less for the poor. The percentage of the population under fifteen was nearly double what it is today. Yet even the small number of aged poor were in dire straits, dependent upon charity for subsistence in their old age. The system of poor relief, once more a local responsibility, encouraged Justices of the Peace to fix wage rates at the lowest level possible. Employers needed little encouragement, since where relief was necessary the burden fell upon all rate-payers more or less equally to provide the funds. The state was reluctant to assume the burden of relief of poverty. The Poor Law was a minimum framework, designed to provide just enough employment to discourage disorder. So it was left almost entirely to private initiative to provide such charity as it could afford and, as in the previous century, it was the merchant classes, again particularly in London, which responded, together with the Puritan section of the gentry. This charity was again of a tangible nature providing schools, almshouses, credit for apprentices, all measures which had the effect of re-moulding society along the lines favoured by the philanthropists; of crucial importance during the power struggle to come.

In 1610 at Greatham, now in the county of Cleveland, Bishop Stichill of Durham's Hospital of God, St. Mary and St. Cuthbert of 1272 was refounded although it was rebuilt again in 1803 by James Wyatt (1746-1813) under the patronage of the Duke of Bridgewater. The hospital to this day houses elderly and infirm clergymen, known as brothers and is run by a master who is also the vicar of the nearby parish church (Plate 29). Three years later in 1613 Edward Alyn, the actor-manager owner of the Fortune Playhouse, laid the foundation stone for his College of God's Gift, which later became known as Dulwich College. It was not opened until 1619, providing accommodation for six poor men and six poor women, together with a school for the education of twelve boys. The school has long since disappeared but the almshouse is still there, a beautiful cream coloured building at the corner of Gallery Road and College Road, Dulwich in South London (Plate 30). Henry Howard, Earl of Northampton, built three groups of almshouses in 1614, all quadrangular in plan; at Clun (Salop), at Castle Rising (Norfolk), and at Greenwich. Plans of the last two are shown in Figures 38 and 39.

Sir Thomas Coningsby, a friend of Sir Philip Sydney, founded a hospital for twelve old men and a chaplain at Hereford in 1614. The accommodation, half for retired soldiers or marines and half for Sir Thomas' own retainers, was built round a small courtyard, utilising for the chapel and dining room buildings originally belonging to the Knights of St. John of Jerusalem. The inmates had quaint military style uniforms, which they wear to this day on ceremonial occasions, the senior man being known as the Corporal of Coningsby's Company of Servitors. The plan of Coningsby's Hospital is shown in Figure 40.

Perhaps the most delightful group built during this period is the charmingly named Nappers' Mite in the town centre of Dorchester in Dorset. Provided under the will of Sir Robert Napier in 1615, the almshouses provided seven single-storey dwellings around a small court-yard, the upper storey at the front over the arcaded walkway being the audit room. The central gable now sports a large clock supported on an iron bracket which was a later addition. The accommodation provided proved to be far too small by modern day standards and the old folk are now housed in more suitably sized homes elsewhere. However, the buildings live on under a new use as a cafe, members of the public now being able to sit out in the courtyard as did many generations of almsfolk during the last three hundred and seventy years (Plate 31).

Abbott's Hospital at Guildford and Sackville College, East Grinstead,

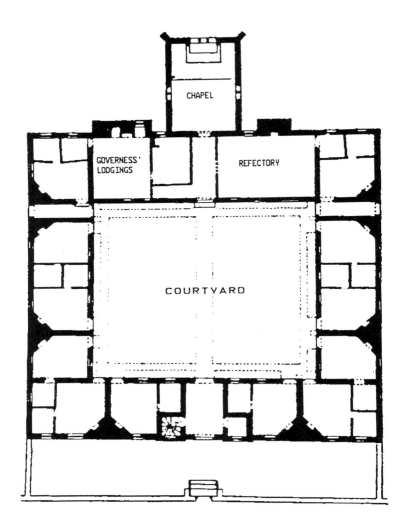

*Fig 38. Plan of Trinity Hospital,
Castle Rising, Norfolk.*

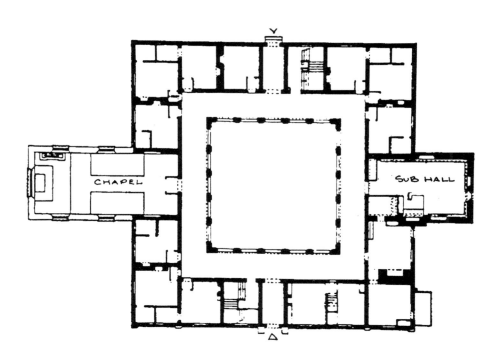

*Fig 39. Plan of Trinity Hospital,
Greenwich, London.*

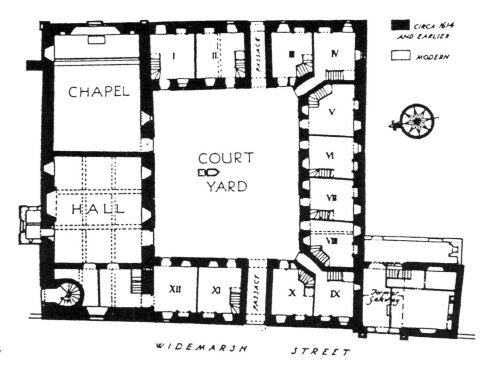

*Fig 40. Plan of Coningsby's Hospital,
Hereford, Hereford and Worcester.*

were both built in 1617, the former of brick with a Tudoresque entrance
gateway, having staircase turrets, each capped with a lead cupola; the
latter, founded by the second Earl of Dorset, of sandstone with tall,
mullioned windows to the special accommodation provided within for the
Dorset family (Plate 32).

Finally, in this early Stuart period, mention must be made of the
picturesque group founded by an unknown wool merchant in the village
of Moretonhampstead on the edge of Dartmoor (Plate 33). Built out of
square blocks of granite at the front, with mullioned windows at the eaves
level under a thatched roof, the almshouses, like Nappers' Mite mentioned
earlier, have a loggia with turned stone columns supporting the eleven
semi-circular arches of the arcade. The dwellings no longer house
almspeople, who have been re-housed in more modern accommodation
across the way. However, the buildings are well looked after since they are
now in the ownership of the National Trust.

Then came the Civil War and its aftermath. Much has been written of
the causes of the Civil War, and it would serve little or no purpose to relate
them in detail here, save to highlight their effects upon the subject matter
in question – the provision of hospitals and almshouses.

The reasons were many and complex, but can be distilled down to
basically three, religious, constitutional and economic; religious because
of Charles' overt Catholicism, anathema to the Protestant Church of
England; constitutional because of Charles' refusal to accept the role of
Parliament in government; and economic because of Charles' interference
in trade by the granting of monopolies to minority groups, his abuse of the
Court of Wards to divert funds to his own use, his arbitrary fines and
confiscation of funds entrusted to the Crown for safety, forced loans, and
above all his levying of Ship Money from inland towns.

The furore which attended his excesses culminated in almost five years of conflict, at the end of which, on 30th January 1649 the king was executed as "a traitor to the good people of England", and a Commonwealth declared with Oliver Cromwell as Lord Protector.

The Rump of the Long Parliament was expelled by Cromwell in April 1653, having introduced few domestic reforms other than to sell off Dean and Chapter lands and the lands of some seven hundred Loyalists. A military government was then summoned, known as the Barebones Parliament, so-called after one of its leaders, a religious zealot called Praise God Barbon. This Parliament lasted only a short time before also being dissolved by Cromwell, who then carved up the country into eleven regions each administered by a major-general. Other parliaments were called during the next seven years, but none could break the power of the generals. It took the courage of General Monck and the tenacity of the City of London to break their grip, and in desperation, to invite Charles II to return as king.

Very few almshouses were founded during the Commonwealth period. Ingram's Hospital in Bootham, York was built in 1640 by Sir William Ingram, for the deserving poor of the town, utilising an old Norman archway beneath a square battlemented tower from the nearby Holy Trinity Priory as the entrance porch to the chapel which stands in the centre of the row of dwellings (Plate 34). Also built in 1640 were Henry Cornish's Almshouses at Chipping Norton (Plate 35). Multi-gabled and built of Cotswold stone, the almshouses were enclosed within a substantial wall with a wrought-iron gateway, as were Drake's Almshouses at Amersham in Buckinghamshire where the almshouses, originally six in number, form three sides of a tiny quadrangle, the fourth side comprising the screen-wall and gate.

For Charles II, the Commonwealth had not existed; he discounted the eleven years of the Interregnum and dated his reign from the death of his father, 30th January 1649. Various Acts of Parliament were speedily passed, mainly to provide him with an income in lieu of the Purveyance and revenue from the Court of Wards. He received an income of £100,000, mainly from an excise on beer, cider and tea, and £1 million was voted by Parliament to pay for the army. An act of Indemnity was passed, pardoning all offences arising from the Civil War and its aftermath, apart that is from the signatories to his father's death warrant. But of the fifty or so arraigned for that, just over half were condemned and only eleven executed. Confiscated lands of Royalist supporters were in the main restored, although several thousand Catholic landowners were disappointed, particularly in Ireland.

In religious matters a strict Church of England regime was imposed, excluding non-conformists and of course Catholics from any share of the affairs of central and local government under the Clarendon Code of Statutes, the Corporation Act 1661, the Act of Uniformity 1662, the Conventicle Act 1664 and the Five Mile Act 1665. However the king who, in 1662 had married Catherine of Braganza, secretly declared himself a Catholic to his friend and mentor, Louis XIV of France, and promised to re-introduce the Catholic religion when the time was opportune. In return for this declaration, he received financial assistance from France for the whole of his reign.

Throughout the reign of Charles the country was more or less at war with Holland, although surprisingly enough a marriage was arranged between William, Prince of Orange (1650-1702) and Mary (1662-94), the daughter of James, Duke of York. In the closing years of the reign, local government was remodelled to produce parliamentary electorates and juries favourably disposed to the king. Particularly under the new order, Charles imposed upon the City of London the rule that no Lord Mayor, Sheriff or Recorder could be appointed without royal approval. As a result of this, after Charles' death in 1685, his brother James II (1633-1701) succeeded peacefully. Indeed the two risings which took place soon after, that of the Earl of Argyll in Scotland and the Duke of Monmouth, Charles' illegitimate son, in Dorset, had little or no support and were very soon put down. Both leaders were executed and savage reprisals followed. Judge Jeffrey's Bloody Assizes in the south-west after Monmouth's defeat at Sedgemoor became particularly notorious.

During his three year reign, James tried every avenue to install Catholics into high office, ignoring the Test Act of 1673 which sought to test office-holders' allegiance to the Church of England. Opposition was fierce, fuelled by news of Louis XIV's persecution of French Protestants, but despite that, James installed the Papist Earl of Tyrconnel as Lord Lieutenant of Ireland, Sir Roger Strickland, also a Papist, as Lord High Admiral, Lord Arundell of Wardour as Lord Privy Seal, and Edward Petre, a Jesuit, as a member of the Privy Council. The chief minister, Sunderland, also declared himself to be a Catholic, although not until June 1688. Further "remodelling" of local government was planned and the Court of Commissioners for Ecclesiastical Causes imposed Catholics upon the colleges of Oxford and Cambridge.

In 1687 James issued a Declaration of Indulgences, which suspended the Test Acts and allowed freedom of religious practice to Protestants and Catholics, and followed it a year later with a reaffirmation, sending dissenting bishops to the Tower.

The last straw was when his queen bore him a son, James Edward, which ensured that the king's attempts, during his lifetime, to restore the Catholic religion to the state would be continued indefinitely. As a result, an invitation was sent to William of Orange to invade England signed by seven Englishmen, including the Bishop of London, the Earl of Danby, a Sydney, a Russell and a Cavendish.

James back-pedalled immediately, replacing Catholic appointees with Protestant, and annulling all municipal charters granted since 1679 which had favoured the Catholic cause. But all to no avail. William landed at Brixham in November 1688 with 11,000 foot soldiers and 4,000 horse, and the whole of the country went over to his side, led by James' younger daughter Princess Anne. James fled to France with his wife and son Charles Edward, who was to provide, over the next fifty years or so, colourful interludes in English history.

Royalty's contribution to the provision of almshouses was specialised and monumental; specialised because provision was made for aged servicemen only and monumental because the buildings provided were first and foremost prestigious reminders of the munificence of the Crown, architectural masterpieces, the Crown's tangible contribution to civic design. Charles II's sojourn on the Continent during the years of the Commonwealth had of course exposed him to the influence of the court of Louis XIV (1638-1715), its lavish lifestyle and the emerging Renaissance architecture carried out on a scale which, although relatively common on mainland Europe, had never been experienced in England because of the Puritan regime. Louis' contribution to the building of Paris was a spectacular achievement, brought about, not so much by the genius for design of the newly emerging architectural profession, but by its ability to organise the construction of large, complex structures, together with the total control of the environment of the city. Prior to that, the guilds of builders and carpenters had a stranglehold on all new construction, the elements of which had a scale which reflected the relatively modest resources of the individual members. It took the breadth of vision and resources of the Sun King himself and his cohorts to produce architecture on a scale which had been experienced previously only in the building of the great cathedrals during the Gothic period.

Royal patronage in France during this period took the form of several large institutions for the poor. Two notable ones were the Hospital de la Salpetrière, begun in 1656 and completed in 1668, and L'Hôtel de Mars ou des Invalides commenced in 1674, with the inmates moving in, in 1676. Both buildings were designed by Liberal Bruant, son of Sebastian Bruant, "Général de Bâtiments (buildings), Ponts (bridges) et Chaussées (roadways) de France. The Hospital de la Salpetrière was an asylum or workhouse, which was actually in use until the twentieth century and housed over 7,800 persons during its heyday.

In 1663 Bruant succeeded his father as "Maistre des Oeuvres de Charpentiers pour avoir l'oeil sur tous les charpentiers des maisons royales", and "Architecte du Roi", and eleven years later was entrusted with the building of L'Hôtel de Mars ou des Invalides which the king had commissioned for "les estropiez, vieux et caducs soldats" (crippled, old and decrepit soldiers) who had until then been housed in monasteries. The edict for the foundation of the hospital, dated 1674, recites; "qu'il estoit bien raisonable que ceux de cette monarchie.....jouissent du repos qu'ils ont assuré à nos autres sujets, et passaient le reste de leurs jours en tranquillité." The design took the form of a central court known as La Cour Royale which was 290 feet by 190 feet and flanked by two smaller courts on either side, each 138 feet by 120 feet. Within the Cour Royale, opposite the main entrance, Bruant placed his chapel, the Soldiers' Church, a considerable building some 192 feet by 72 feet. Later Mansard attached his Church of the Dome at the farthest end, separated from the chapel proper by the high altar. On either side of the chapel and separated from it by long, narrow courts, were large projecting enclosures of long buildings, with the one to the east containing the infirmary and the one to the west a priest's garden and cloister-garth with miscellaneous administrative buildings.

The whole composition was symmetrical in design and uniform in treatment, except for the Cour Royale which had two lofty arcaded galleries running around the sides of the court and elaborate ornamentation. The remaining main buildings were of four storeys with dormers in the roofs. Plate 36 shows an aerial view of the hospital today. On either side of the Cour Royale were the refectories for the old soldiers with separate mess rooms for officers and other ranks. On the outer side of the four smaller courts were ranged the soldiers' rooms, each wing having a central corridor with cubicles leading off. The Governor's residence occupied the left hand end of the entrance front, the resident surgeon occupying quarters at the opposite end, each with its own separate offices and stables. The whole complex was provided with ample staircases which, together with the corridors, gave efficient vertical and lateral accessibility. The arrangement of the infirmaries was straightforward, with wards 22 feet wide running round the outer sides of the courts, two corridors dividing four courts with the octagonal spaces at the junctions.

Paris obviously was not as urban in those days as it is now; the hospital was in fact in the countryside, and was designed to be self-contained, with ample cellars, and the whole of the fourth floor given over to granaries for the storage of corn. It had its own water supply, the well being taken down 10 feet below the bed of the adjoining river to a depth of some 63 feet and lined with stone. The pump, worked by three mules, supplied a huge lead cistern from which the whole of the hospital was supplied through lead pipes.

The elevational treatment is thought by many architectural historians to be inferior in execution to the plan, the worst feature being the prodigious archway, some 42 feet wide above the main entrance. This arch supported really nothing at all, breaking the roof in a most unpleasant manner.

Mansard supplanted Bruant as architect when the building was nearing completion and, ignoring his predecessor's concepts, added the "meaningless and vainglorious" Church of the Dome.

Les Invalides was the last serious effort at any great public improvement to Paris made by Louis XIV but, as intimated above, it had a profound influence on the court of Charles II both in England and as it turned out, in Ireland also.

James Butler, the Duke of Ormonde, spent the years of exile with Charles II in Paris and, upon the Restoration was made firstly Lord Lieutenant and later Viceroy of Ireland, based in Dublin. With the precedent of Les Invalides in mind, the idea of an asylum for aged and disabled veterans was first considered in the 1670s by the Earl of Grenard and the Earl of Essex. In 1679 the king agreed to a levy on Irish military pay, the proceeds of which were to be devoted to the erection of a building to be used as an asylum for those: "..who by reason of age, wounds or other infirmities since their first coming into Our army, are grown unfit to be any longer continued in Our service." Ormonde wished the hospital, his first venture in Ireland, to be on a grand scale, classical in layout and Continental in style, for although he needed a home for pensioners, he also wanted a building of distinction which would mark Dublin's debut as a city of European standing.

William Robinson, the Surveyor General of Ireland was consulted and a site in the village of Kilmainham near to Phoenix Park on the outskirts of the city was selected, on which were the ruins of the Preceptory of the Knights Hospitaller. The design was duly approved by Ormonde and the foundation stone laid in April 1680. The new building was to be so spectacular it was suggested that Trinity College in the city should move there and that the hospital should be transferred to the college's existing buildings in College Green, as ".. the Hospital would make a magnificent college and being out of town would be free from those mischiefs that now attend it". The Hospital was completed at the end of 1686 at a cost of £23,500 and dedicated to the martyr, Charles I.

Kilmainham Hospital, originally housing 300 old men, is much smaller than Les Invalides, having only one courtyard, instead of seven in Paris. The courtyard is surrounded on three sides by arcades, the fourth originally having been arcaded except for the central five bays of the dining room. The enlarged master's lodge and the passage adjoining the chapel encroach onto the loggia in the north-west and north-east corners (see plan in Figure 41).

From the outside the façades appear large and institutional with the steeply pitched roofs and dormers, reminiscent of the formal French Renaissance style. Inside the courtyard however, the effect changes to a more domestic scale and character on three sides with the more formal classical portico of the Great Hall on the fourth. There is a strong sense of symmetry, the main axis running from the main entrance on the south façade, through the centre of the Great Hall and spire, and beyond, through the formal gardens. To the south, the perspective closes on the gatehouse in Kilmainham village. The focal point of the courtyard is the Great Hall with its wall mounted and still functioning sundial and clock tower with weather-vane. The domestic buildings were, for the period, pleasant and reasonably private, each room housing four men with a fireplace, musket rack and privy cubicle. The most infirm pensioners lived on the ground floor, the officers had suites on the first floor, with the remainder on the top floor. Meals were taken in the Great Hall and each

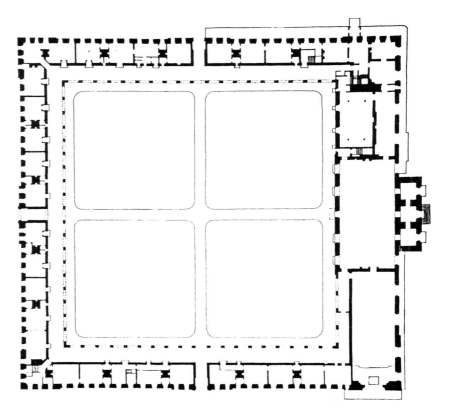

Fig 41. Plan of Kilmainham Hospital, Dublin.

day the inmates attended services in the magnificent chapel. The institution gradually took on a military function, the main front becoming the official residence of the commander-in-chief of the army in Ireland. Many ceremonial functions took place there and it was visited by royalty. It was handed over to the Republic in 1922 and ceased to function as an almshouse in 1928. The buildings were used as the Garda headquarters until the early 1980s when extensive restoration works were undertaken to convert them into a National Centre for Culture and the Arts. Plate 37 shows an aerial view of the courtyard.

With the examples of Les Invalides and Kilmainham, and whilst the latter was under construction, Charles in 1682 commissioned the building of the Royal Hospital at Chelsea, although owing to mismanagement by Lord Ranelagh, the Hospital Treasurer, the building was not completed until 1692. Christopher Wren, Charles' Surveyor-General of Works, was entrusted with the original design, although extensions were added in later centuries by Robert Adam, Sir John Soane and Sir John Vanbrugh. Like Louis XIV, Charles founded the hospital for veterans of the regular army who had become unfit for duty, either because of old age (they had to have served at least twenty years with the colours) or as a result of wounds. Originally the asylum was provided with only one quadrangle, but with the increase in the size of the standing army by James II and William III, provision had to be made in later years for a greater number of in-pensioners, and further accommodation was provided in two other courts.

Charles himself had very little money to spare, and received no support from his Government. A notable exception was the Paymaster General, Sir Stephen Fox, who as well as providing substantial funds out of his own pocket, organised a subvention of army pay, as in Ireland, which was the hospital's main source of revenue until 1847, since when it has been supported by Parliamentary votes. The site chosen comprised an area of some thirty acres upon which had once stood the Chelsea College, an intended theological institution founded by James I. Three open courts were provided, mainly by Wren, the principal one, Figure Court, with the statue of Charles I in the centre, being the most important architecturally, containing the Great Hall and Chapel, together with the principal pensioners' wards. Figure 42 shows a plan of the hospital. Plate 38 shows a view of the Figure Court.

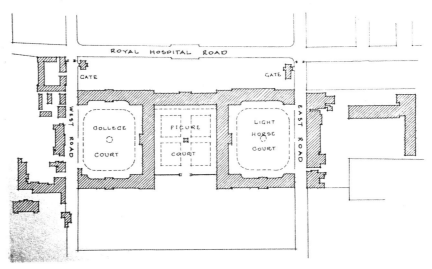

Fig 42. Plan of the Royal Hospital, Chelsea, London.

William and Mary were declared joint rulers in February 1689 by Act of Parliament and under the Act of Settlement of 1701, the succession was fixed, failing heirs, to Mary's sister Anne, and after that to the House of Hanover, descendants of Charles I's sister Elizabeth and the Elector Palatine.

Almost the first of William's priorities was the subjugation of Ireland which, with the exception of Londonderry, had briefly been liberated from British rule following the revolt of Irish Catholic peers. Starting with the Battle of the Boyne in July 1690, William's campaign was as successful as Cromwell's fifty years earlier. The upstart Catholic Patriot's Parliament was annulled and all but a handful of the Irish population was excluded from all public offices.

England and the Netherlands were now allied against France where party divisions had prevented the latter from dominating European trade and, together with Spain, had ejected the Dutch from the Spanish Netherlands.

However, following William's death in 1702, Anne's general, John Churchill, Duke of Marlborough (1650-1722), placed Britain in a commanding position as a result of victories at Blenheim (1704), Ramillies (1706), Oudenaarde (1708), and Malplaquet (1709). By the time of the queen's death in 1714, England was established as the most formidable emergent country in the civilised world.

Following Charles II's examples of hospitals for soldiers at Kilmainham and Chelsea, William and Mary perceived a need to provide for their retired seamen. The Queen's House at Greenwich had been designed by Inigo Jones (1573-1652) in the Palladian style for Charles I's queen, Henrietta Maria. After the Restoration the Queen Mother again took up residence there and Greenwich became one of Charles II's favourite haunts. So fond was he of it that he decided to build a residence there, and commissioned John Webb, Inigo Jones' pupil and nephew to pull down the mediaeval Palace of Placentia and build a replacement on the site. When his niece Mary was looking for a site for her new hospital for retired seamen, Webb's building, now known as the King's House, seemed ideal.

The hospital was founded by Royal Charter in October 1694 and at first had only modest pretensions as it had charitable status. Its purpose was entirely related to the relief of aged seamen and their dependants. Like Les Invalides, the building acquired a quality which had not been anticipated when it was commissioned. Sir Christopher Wren became the Surveyor of Works and was so enthusiastic that he gave his services free of charge. His first design had a magnificence not seen previously in secular English architecture. The plan had a Baroque arrangement of narrowing courts leading to its central feature which was a vast chapel with dome in the style of St. Paul's. Queen Mary was overwhelmed by its monumentality and was unhappy because it obscured the Queen's House. Moreover, she wished that the King's House should remain intact. She decreed that a corridor of land be left some 115 feet wide between the Queen's House and the river.

Wren's final design compromised on the central chapel by splitting it in two – a smaller chapel and a dining hall with each having its own cupola facing the other across a narrow court, with the Queen's House further up the hill on the central axis.

Wren was succeeded as Surveyor of Works by Sir John Vanbrugh (1664-1726). Unusually, the foundations of all the blocks were laid at the same time, in 1696. The King's House renamed King Charles' House, was refurbished as the chapel and its twin, the King William Block, which was the refectory, was the first new building to be completed. This contained the Painted Hall, perhaps the most famous Baroque room outside Italy. Both buildings had smaller brick-built blocks alongside, but they were caught up in the growing monumentality of the composition and were eventually rebuilt to match the Webb design, giving added emphasis to the Palladian Court.

John Evelyn was the hospital's first treasurer and succeeded in raising £7,000 within a month of his taking office. Although Queen Mary died shortly after the Royal Charter was proclaimed, King William was determined to see the project through and as well as donating the royal buildings and the grounds to the hospital, gave £2,000 to the building fund.

The first pensioners took up residence in 1705, some eleven years after the original charter was granted, although their numbers did not reach 1,000 for a further generation. Its full capacity of 3,000 was not reached until the later 18th century.

From the first, there were complaints that the needs of the pensioners were subjugated to the aspirations of the architects. Both Vanbrugh and Nicholas Hawksmoor considered that the hospital would not be completed until it had a central feature and repeatedly produced amendments to the plan, each one more extravagant than the last. Indeed a minute of the Fabric Committee dated sometime in 1717 complained:

"the Board, taking notice that the Managers of Works do contrive and execute designs, as well in the outward buildings as in the disposition of the inside, without consulting or advising with the Board. Resolved that whoever shall for the future undertake any schemes or proceed in any work without the approval of the Board first, shall defray the charge of all the works at their own expense."

The distinguished members of the Board were originally chosen with a view to their fund-raising abilities, but their influence on the increasingly grandiose design was more noticeable. Hardly had Hawksmoor finished the inside of the Hall than James Thornhill was appointed to paint it – and it took him nineteen years to complete the project! Even after having waited such an inordinately long time for their refectory, the poor pensioners were banished to the floor below. The room was considered to be much too grandiose for them to use. Indeed, Dr.Johnson, after a visit to Greenwich in 1763 wrote: "The buildings of Greenwich are too magnificent for a place of charity," and Peter the Great is reputed to have suggested to King William that he convert St James' into a hospital and move his court to Greenwich.

In the 1860s, over a century and a half after its foundation, when its numbers had again decreased to under half its capacity, a Royal Commission was instituted to enquire into the many allegations of corruption and maladministration. It decided to close the institution and in 1873 the Royal Naval College was transferred to the hospital buildings from Portsmouth. Plate 39 shows a view of the hospital painted in 1755 by Canaletto.

Another of Wren's masterpieces, again an almshouse, lies less than two miles from the Royal Hospital. Morden College is approached from a narrow footpath leading from the south-east corner of Blackheath.

Founded in 1695 by Sir John Morden to accommodate "poor honest, sober and discreet merchants who shall have lost all their estates by accidents and perils of the seas, or by any other accidents, ways or means, in their honest endeavour to get their living by way of merchandising", the college accommodates forty-four pensioners in four ranges around a beautifully proportioned courtyard with the usual refectory and chapel. The chapel contains woodcarvings by Grinling Gibbons, fine stained glass and a six-sided pulpit. The design is all that one would expect of Wren, brick and tile with stone dressings and colonnades to the courtyard reminiscent of Chelsea.

Salisbury is particularly well-endowed with almshouses, as might be expected from a cathedral city, having no less than fourteen separate groups dating from mediaeval times until the present-day. We have already encountered St. Nicholas' Hospital, built in 1214, in an earlier chapter. Two more, however, stand out as masterpieces of the Renaissance; Trinity Hospital of 1702, typical of the courtyard design (Plate 40) and the magnificent College Matrarum, built for the widows of the clergy in 1682. Standing just within the cathedral precincts, this is Sir Christopher Wren at his best in the domestic scale, with classical proportions, a fine pediment and cupola over (Plate 41).

William and Mary died without issue and were succeeded by Mary's younger sister Anne (1665-1714), although she did not reign for very long. During the twelve years that she did, very few almshouses of note were built. Berkeley Hospital, Worcester (Plate 42), and the Fishermen's Hospital Great Yarmouth (Plate 43) were both completed during her reign, having been commenced during the reign of her sister. However, two London almshouses of this period stand out as being exceptional. The Ironmongers' Almshouses in Kingsland Road, Shoreditch, were built by Sir Richard Geffrye in 1710. The twenty-eight two-storey almshouses form three sides of an open square with the chapel occupying the centre of the main range with pediment, bell tower and a statue of the founder in a niche over the entrance hall. Although no longer used as almshouses, the London County Council, when it was in existence, preserved the buildings as a museum of London domestic architecture, and as the Geffrye Museum it is now a well-known centre for the study of building materials and methods from bygone ages. Trinity Almshouses, Mile End Road, actually founded in 1695, are attributed to Wren and were built for the Corporation of Trinity House, like so many others throughout the country, as a home for retired seamen. Two rows of single-storey almshouses, twelve on one side, eleven on the other, face each other across a narrow, slightly tapering, grassed courtyard with a delightful little chapel with pediment, clock tower, cupola and weather-vane closing the vista at the narrow end. At the other, the Mile End Road frontage, the difference between the odd and even number of dwellings is made up by a serpentine brick wall with wrought-iron gates between the pedimented gables of the cottages, each with sundry commemorative plaques and maritime impedimenta, including two model ships carved out of marble. Figure 43 shows a plan of almshouses as constructed and Plate 44 a view of the courtyard today.

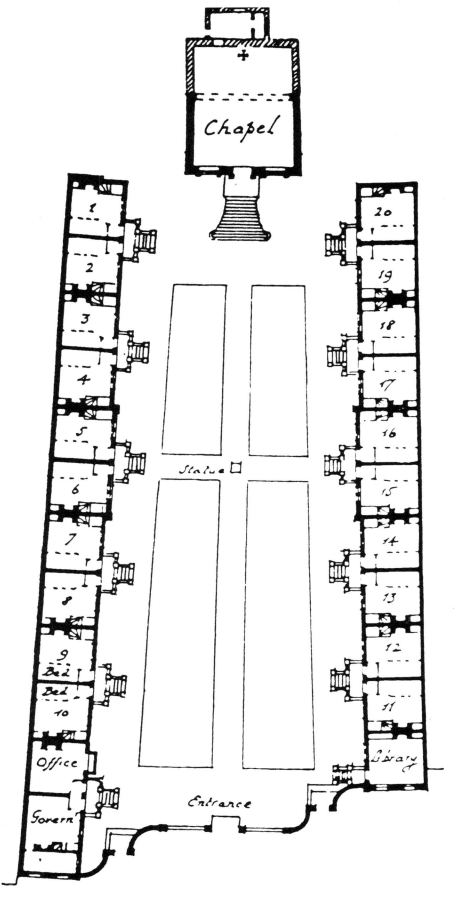

Fig 43. Plan of Trinity Almshouses,
Mile End Road, London.

Plate 29. Greatham Hospital, Cleveland.

Plate 30. Dulwich College, South London.

114

Plate 31. Napper's Mite, Dorchester, Dorset.

Plate 32. Sackville College, East Grinstead, West Sussex.

Plate 33. Moretonhampstead Almshouses, Devon.

Plate 34. *Ingram's Hospital, Bootham, York.*

Plate 35. *Henry Cornish's Almshouses, Chipping Norton, Oxfordshire.*

117

Plate 36. Les Invalides, Paris, France.

Plate 37. Kilmainham Hospital, Dublin, Ireland.

118

Plate 38. Royal Hospital, Chelsea, London.

Plate 39. View of the Royal Naval Hospital, Greenwich, London, painted by Canaletto, 1755.

Plate 40. Trinity Hospital, Salisbury, Wiltshire.

Plate 41. College Matrarum, Salisbury, Wiltshire.

Plate 42. Berkeley Hospital, Worcester, Hereford and Worcester.

Plate 43. Fishermen's Hospital, Great Yarmouth, Norfolk.

Plate 44. Trinity Almshouses, Mile End Road, London.

Chapter 9

The Georgian Period

Unlike the rest of Europe in the eighteenth century, government in England flowed from the shires to the capital and not vice versa as applies today. The Revolutionary Settlement of 1680 had guaranteed power to the landed gentry which was endorsed by small business and the farmers, the so-called middling folk, for although the latter had little love for the carriage folk, they abhorred all the more the interference of central government, particularly the imposition of taxes, military levies or corn bounty.

The effect of such regional chauvinism was to produce a totally material system of local government with such anomalies as County Durham, virtually ruled by its Prince Bishop, Haverfordwest in Pembrokeshire which, like London, had its own Lord Lieutenant and Keeper of the Roles, and Beccles in Suffolk which was governed by the owner of its Fen. Large, growing industrial towns, particularly in the north were still run by the manorial courts which had served them since mediaeval times. In 1750, Halifax in the West Riding of Yorkshire although having a population of over 50,000, had no Justices of the Peace of its own. Manchester was governed by its court leet and higher up the legal scale, private and manorial courts continued to administer their own quaint interpretations of the law in regard to byelaws, nuisance and disputes over land and property.

Moreover, when improvements and amenities were introduced such as street lighting, paving and policing, these were introduced by private initiatives; self-help rather than as a result of centrally agreed policies.

The great landowners and merchants exerted tremendous power as employers – there were of course no recognised trade unions until much later. Patronage also purchased considerable power and the local offices controlled by the local top brass and backed up by law dictated the destinies of local folk. At the top of the pile was the Lord Lieutenant of the County, the Crown's representative at shire level. The Lord Lieutenant appointed the Justices of the Peace, the Clerks of the Peace, an appointment for life, and commanded the local militia. Central government's directives were passed down through his office and beneath him, his Sheriffs and their deputies carried out similar functions at the lower level. However, the office with the greatest effect on every day life was that of Justice of the Peace, the holders of which wielded wide and almost unsupervised power over local communities. Acting on their own, JPs issued warrants for arrest and punished scores of misdemeanours such as drunkenness, vagrancy and profanity. In dealing with poachers particularly, they often were dealing with offences against their own property, a situation which today would not be tolerated as a conflict of interest. But in the early eighteenth century no heed was paid to such niceties and the miscreants were whipped, fined or sent to the house of correction. For those who committed more serious crimes such as stealing or assault, they were sent for trial at the quarter sessions. JPs working in pairs could exercise summary justice over ale-houses, paternity suits, runaway servants and apprentices, and could commit suspects for trial at county assizes which took place twice a year as judges perambulated the country. Such courts had power of life or death and increasingly as the eighteenth century bore on, of transportation for life. JPs fixed wages and prices, regulated apprenticeships, swore in local constables and oversaw markets and fairs. In administering the Poor Law they made settlements, conducted examinations and ordered the removal of those judged not to be entitled to receive local relief.

Although JPs wielded great power in rural areas, in the towns the growing means of local administration was the corporation. Most great regional centres such as York, Exeter and Coventry were incorporated and exercised wide regulatory powers over residents, levying rates and rents, managing land and property, licensing markets and fairs and, most important from our study's point of view, administering charities. Urban Justices of the Peace or magistrates, passed local byelaws and saw to their adherence, and in an age when parliamentary representation was becoming increasingly important, they controlled the local franchises.

The City of London was the most important and prestigious. Government within the city was split between the twenty-six aldermen elected for life, who comprised the upper court, and the two hundred and thirty-four freemen, elected annually from the city livery companies. The city council elected its own sheriffs, and commanded its own militia. We have seen in previous chapters how crucial that privilege had proved to be in the affairs of the country. In the eighteenth century over 12,000 Londoners voted in elections for aldermen and councillors.

But the bedrock of all local government was the parish, or in the cities, the vestry, of which there were of the order of 10,000 throughout the country. Parishes were run by officers appointed by the Justices of the Peace or increasingly, by ratepayers. These officers were the churchwardens, the constables, the surveyors of the highways, the overseers of the poor, even the pinder who kept the animal pound. Local worthies were forced sometimes against their will to take on these duties for two years. They were unpaid and thankless tasks and were often passed on to others after payment of a fee. They were at times, also unpopular with the locals. For instance, the surveyor of highways had a right to six days unpaid labour a year from each parishioner to help with road repairs and construction.

The hangover from mediaeval times meant that local government bumbled on, quite unsuitable to the needs of a growing economy. As a result, where public authority would not address a particular need, private enterprise stepped in to fill the breach. Private utilities were set up following the passing of private acts of parliament and special rates could be levied to pay for such amenities as sewerage, water supplies and turnpike roads.

As in previous centuries, private funds were used to provide dispensaries and medical hospitals as well as the more usual charities, almshouses and schools. Conciliation courts were set up to settle disagreements over small debts and other money disputes.

But the ongoing problem of poverty and the poor was, as in previous administrations, the bugbear of authority. England was almost unique in having a poor law at all. Elsewhere in Europe, especially in Catholic countries such as Ireland, relief was still looked upon as almsgiving to be administered by the church, or care by the extended family. As was noted in previous chapters, an administrative system existed which, particularly since the Act of Settlement and Removal of 1662, confirmed that relief of poverty was to be at the smallest unit of local administration, the parish. The 1662 Poor Law defined responsibility for each pauper which was administered with regard to 'settlement'. Everyone was deemed to have a settlement in one, and only one, parish. Such a settlement, a typically English property right, could be established in one of several ways: a) by birth in a particular parish, b) having a father settling there, c) by marrying a husband there, d) by being hired as a servant for at least one year there, e) by being apprenticed there, or f) by renting a dwelling-house there. A person looking for relief by reason of illness, destitution or incapacity for work could look only to the parish in which he or she had a settlement, and no other. This policy had the obvious merit of defining responsibility for relief in a cogent way which it would be difficult to refute. However, it also had the disbenefit of keeping workers in or near their settlement parish. Strictly speaking, a person needed a certificate to leave his parish to seek work elsewhere. Paupers wore a 'P' badge on their clothing and officers in charge had the right, in fact the duty, to drive back to their native parishes, vagrants and all those without relief was concerned.

On the other hand, this exclusive policy had its benefits. Paupers who hailed from the parish engendered some sympathy from their neighbours and from the overseers of the poor, who made sure that they did not actually starve, and indeed in many ways made life as comfortable as could be expected for those who had fallen on hard times.

Those who had no settlement were relentlessly driven from the parish .The poor, the old and the sick were all ejected or in some cases bribed to move on. Unmarried pregnant women were treated particularly badly; if they gave birth in the parish then their offspring would immediately be entitled to settlement.

The cost of poor relief accelerated at an alarming rate during the eighteenth century. In 1700 it was estimated to be £600,000; by 1776 it had risen to £1.5 million and by 1803 it was a staggering £4.2 million. Part of these funds went towards relief for the sick, the old and the unemployed. But increasingly, it went to topping up the income of workers on rock-bottom wages, to support their families or to help out during periods of only seasonal employment. The Speenhamland ruling of 1795 linked topping-up to inflation and imposed an intolerable burden on those responsible for raising the cash who were usually the magistrates.

The ratepayers resented the poor, considering them to be feckless, naturally idle and who worked as little as possible. Spare cash would be spent on drinking and debauchery. Defoe complained:

"When wages are good they won't work any more than from hand to mouth; or if they do work they spend it in riot or luxury, so that it turns to no account to them. Again, as soon as trade receives a check, what follows? Why, then they grow clamorous and noisy, mutinous and saucy another way, and in the meantime they disperse, run away and leave their families upon the parishes to wander about in beggary and distress."

As previously, magistrates believed that wages should be kept low to keep labourers at work longest; to make them more industrious is to "lay them under the necessity of labouring all the time they can spare from rest and sleep". Keeping the workers only an inch or two from penury meant that as soon as they became ill or there was a downturn in the economy, they and their families were on the parish. They were never able to save anything that would tide them over bad times. Furthermore, there was but a whisker, in financial terms, between working and being on the parish. Indeed, institutionalised paupers generally ate better than families where the breadwinner was in work.

The answer, first tried in 1697 in Bristol, was the workhouse, described by Jeremy Bentham as "a mill to grind rogues honest and idle men industrious".

The workhouse was based on the principle that "if you don't work you don't eat". There the poor could be taught useful skills and at the same time earn their keep, thus sparing the ratepayers the responsibility of providing for them. The Knatchbull Act of 1723 endorsed at national level the policy which hitherto had been pursued at local level, giving discretion to magistrates to refuse outdoor relief to those who would not enter a house of industry. The management of the workhouse was, more often than not, put in the hands of private contractors who exploited the inmates unmercifully for their own ends.

A certain Matthew Marryat of Buckinghamshire was, in the 1730s, running as many as thirty houses. Children had a particularly hard time; the infant mortality rate in London workhouses was very high; out of 2,340 children put into workhouses in 1750, only 168 were alive in 1755. But in spite of the theory, workhouses proved to be totally uneconomic and recourse had to be made continuously to support from the rates. By definition, the inmates were the most unproductive, generally women and young children abandoned by their menfolk, the aged, the sick and increasingly the mentally defective. Moreover, the unscrupulous private contractors who ran them were siphoning off any surpluses. In due course, it was realised that the parish was really too small a unit to support a workhouse. So parishes were joined together to form Poor Law Unions with joint houses of industry. Bigger workhouses incurred bigger losses and only a few hundred were founded.

These responses to poverty failed because they tried to cure the symptoms rather than the root cause, and in any case, were local in extent rather than based on a national policy. Thus poverty was seen as a necessary concomitant to progress by many economists. Indeed, Malthus observed that poverty was the fault of the indigent. They bred too quickly. And as Henry Fielding wrote: "so very useless indeed is this heavy (poor law) tax and so wretched its disposition, that it is a question whether the poor or the rich are more dissatisfied....since the plunder of one serves so little to the real advantage of the other."

But what of the almshouses during this period? Generally speaking, Georgian almshouses were modest in size and scale compared to their predecessors, although usually beautifully proportioned as might be expected in this age of elegance. There were a few exceptions, but none to match the Royal Hospital at Greenwich or St. Cross at Winchester.

Despite its small size – there were only six dwellings – few during this period were more impressive than Fountaine's Hospital at Linton-in-Craven in the Yorkshire Dales. This almshouse was founded in 1721 by Richard Fountaine, a local lad made good, the timber merchant supplying materials for the building of Castle Howard. The design is reputed to have been prepared by Sir John Vanbrugh himself whilst working in Yorkshire; it is certainly in his style, massive proportions to the otherwise small dwellings, with central chapel, tower and cupola (Plate 45).

Of the same date are the Rectors' Almshouses in Sunderland, although much more modest in scale, and the charmingly named Wollaston and Pauncefort almshouses in Highgate Village, London. These almshouses were built in 1656 originally by Sir John Wollaston, a goldsmith, and their administration left in the hands of the governors of Highgate School nearby. They were rebuilt in 1722 by one of the school governors, Sir Edward Pauncefort, who added his own name to the almshouses along with the original founder. Although unpretentious, the single-storey dwellings are typical of the domestic architecture of the period.

Alnut's Hospital at Goring Heath in Oxfordshire was built, as in previous centuries, around three sides of a courtyard with the fourth side having the usual screen wall with entrance gate. The eight single-storey dwellings are arranged symmetrically, four on either side of the chapel with, as at Linton, a tower and cupola (Plate 46).

Frome's Blue House of 1726 was originally almshouse and school combined, a central imposing block with arched windows and a lantern on the roof, flanked by less impressive three-storey wings. Originally the central block housed the school – the Bluecoats' School, hence the name – whilst the almsfolk resided in the wings. The school has long since ceased to exist and the whole building is now used as an almshouse.

Perhaps the most curiously built block in the country though is situated at Stidd-under-Langridge in Lancashire, where John Shireburn the local squire built a small block of six cottages in 1728. The stone building consists of five short bays, the central three having semi-circular arches under a curious Dutch gable. The upper floor is approached by a grand central staircase which arrives at a balustraded balcony, the whole composition giving the illusion of a much larger building than is the actual case (Plate 47).

Not far away, at Mitton in Lancashire, a relative, Sir Michael Shireburn built a much more imposing group of ten almshouses, each having two rooms; five on either side of the usual chapel with pediment surmounted by classical urns. The almshouses and the chapel formed three sides of a square, with the fourth closed off by a low balustrading with the entrance in the centre reached by a semi-circular array of fifteen stone steps (Plate 48). The doors of the almshouses bore the names of the local parishes which benefit from the charity. Unusually, this group of almshouses was demolished stone by stone, and rebuilt in the centre of the nearby village of Hurst Green in 1947.

Abingdon, in Oxfordshire, has a major group of almshouses in its churchyard. The earliest, originally known as St Helen's Hospital was founded in 1417 and suppressed in 1546. It was refounded again in 1553 and named Christ's Hospital with thirteen occupants. Known locally as The Long Alley, the sixteenth century building has a long wooden gallery running its whole length on the elevation facing the parish church (Plate 49). In 1707 Charles Twitty added six more single-storey cottages, three for men and three for women, the classical design having a large central pediment with plaques, surmounted by a timber lantern (Plate 50). Then, eleven years later in 1718, Christ's Hospital was extended by the addition of the so-called Brick Alley Almshouses to form the third side of the square with the parish church of St. Helen in the centre. These, the latest almshouses, were a bricklayer's tour de force with classical arches and pediments and balustrading to the first floor walkway (Plate 51).

Nearby, in 1733, Benjamin Tomkin, another local worthy, provided a further group of eight brick-built almshouses with a Dutch influence, four on either side of a narrow alley, at the end of which a classical gateway with pediment and plaque over, led to a garden beyond (Plate 52).

The City of York, as we have already seen, has several groups of almshouses with three or four provided during the Hanoverian period. Mary Wandesford founded an almshouse in 1739 in Bootham for ten poor spinsters "who shall retire from the hurry and noise of the world into a Religious House of Protestant Retirement." The single building is attributable to John Carr of York. It has seven two-storey arched bays with the central three surmounted by a large pediment with a statue of the foundress in a niche in its centre (Plate 53).

Fifty miles or so away to the south in the village of High Ackworth near Pontefract, Mary Lowther in 1741 endowed a low, single-storey row of stone almshouses, recently renovated (Plate 54).

Sarah, Duchess of Marlborough, the wife of the soldier duke endowed a magnificent group at St. Albans in 1733. It was said that it was to ease her conscience in her old age. The buildings were designed in the classical style, as usual on three sides of a lawned courtyard. The main range had a central three bay pediment with a cartouche in its centre. The two wings are much plainer, although well-proportioned.

Plate 45. Fountaine's Hospital, Linton-in-Craven, North Yorkshire.

Plate 46. Alnut's Hospital, Goring Heath, Oxfordshire.

Plate 47. Shireburn Almshouses, Stidd-under-Langridge, Lancashire.

132

Plate 48. Shireburn Hospital, Hurst Green, Lancashire.

Plate 49. Long Alley Almshouses, Abingdon, Oxfordshire.

Plate 50. Twitty's
Almshouses, Abingdon,
Oxfordshire.

Plate 51. Brick Alley
Almshouses, Abingdon,
Oxfordshire.

Plate 52. Tomkin's Almshouses, Abingdon, Oxfordshire.

Plate 53. Mary Wandesford's Almshouses, York, North Yorkshire.

Plate 54. Mary Lowther's Hospital, Ackworth, West Yorkshire.

Chapter 10

Victorian Almshouses

With the Victorian era came the last great age of almshouse building. Of the two thousand or so groups of almshouses currently occupied, it has been estimated that over thirty percent were built during the sixty-nine years of the great queen's reign.

Housing emerged as one of the great social problems of the period as thousands of erstwhile agricultural labourers and their families migrated to the towns looking for work in the new factories. Row upon row of squalid terrace houses were thrown up in the streets surrounding the manufactories with in many cases, several families occupying one house. Crime and disease were rife as these 'rookeries', as they were termed, became the forerunners of the emerging great urban phenomenon, the classic slum. Frederick Engels (1820-95), in one of the great social essays of all time wrote of the slums of Manchester in 1844:

"I might mention that the most disgusting spot of all is one which lies on the Manchester side of the river (Irk). It is situated to the south-west of Oxford Road and is called Little Ireland. It lies in a fairly deep natural depression on the bend of the river and is completely surrounded by tall factories or high banks and embankments covered with buildings. Here lie two groups of about two hundred cottages most of which are built on the back-to-back principle. Some four thousand people, mostly Irish, inhabit this slum. The cottages are very small, old and dirty, while the streets are uneven, partly unpaved, not properly drained and full of ruts. Heaps of refuse, offal and sickening filth are everywhere interspersed with pools of stagnant liquid. The atmosphere is polluted by the stench and is darkened by the thick smoke of a dozen factory chimneys. A horde of ragged women and children swarm about the streets and they are just as dirty as the pigs which wallow happily on the heaps of garbage and in the pools of filth. In short, this horrid little slum affords as hateful and repulsive a spectacle as the worst courts to be found on the banks of the Irk. The inhabitants live in dilapidated cottages, the windows of which are broken and patched with oilskin. The doors and the door posts are broken and rotten. The creatures who inhabit these dwellings and even their dark, wet cellars, and who live confined amidst all this filth and foul air – which cannot be dissipated because of the surrounding lofty buildings – must surely have sunk to the lowest level of humanity. That is the conclusion that must surely be drawn even by any visitor who examines the slum from the outside, without entering any of the dwellings. But his feelings of horror would be intensified if he were to discover that on average twenty people live in each of these little houses, which at the moment consist of two rooms, an attic and a cellar. One privy – and that usually inaccessible – is shared by about one hundred and twenty people. In spite of all the warnings of the doctors and in spite of the alarm caused to the health authorities by the condition of Little Ireland during the cholera epidemic, the condition of this slum is practically the same in this year of grace 1844 as it was in 1831. Dr Kay describes how not only the cellars but even the ground floors of all the houses in this quarter were damp. He states that at one time a number of cellars were filled in with earth and that they were gradually emptied again and had now been re-occupied by the Irish. One particular cellar which lay below the level of the river was continually flooded with water which gushed in through a hole which had been stuffed full of clay. The handloom weaver who lived there had to clean out his cellar every morning and empty the water into the street.....Gaskell estimates that 20,000 people live in the cellars in Manchester proper. This statement is confirmed by an estimate in the Weekly Dispatch 'from official sources' that twelve percent of the workers live in cellars. The number of workers may be taken as 175,000 and twelve percent of this number is 21,000. As there are just as many cellars in the suburbs as in Manchester itself the total number of workers living in cellars in Greater Manchester must be in between 40-50,000. So much for the dwellings of the workers in the large towns..........It may be added that many families which have only one room take in boarders and lodgers, and it is not uncommon for both men and women lodgers to sleep in the same bed as their married hosts. The Report on the Sanitary Condition of the Labouring Population mentions half a dozen cases in Manchester in which a man sleeps not only with his wife but also with his adult sister-in-law..........Common lodging houses too are very numerous in Manchester. Dr Kay stated that in 1831 there were two hundred and sixty-seven of them in the township of Manchester, and since that date their numbers have no doubt considerably increased. As each lodging house accommodates between twenty and thirty persons, the total number sleeping in them on any one night must be between 5-7,000.........In every room five or seven beds are made up on the floor and human beings of both sexes are packed into them indiscriminately....."

For those who had no home nor work and the sick and the aged, there remained only the workhouse. With the emergence of the austere Victorian ethic, the benevolent if somewhat despotic system which had obtained in previous centuries, was replaced by a much more repressive and cruel regime. In 1832, two years after the Swing Riots had been put down, with nineteen men hanged and nearly five hundred transported, a Royal Commission was set up to enquire into the workings of the Poor Law. The report, instead of concerning itself with paupers and vagrants however, concentrated on inadequately paid labourers in counties where the poor rates were used to supplement wages. As mentioned previously, this had become known as the Speenhamland system after the Berkshire parish where the magistrates, in 1795, fixed the level of "outdoor" relief with regard to the current price of bread. In 1832, however, the Commissioners condemned the system, arguing that paupers did not respect their employers if their wages were enhanced by relief. They were discouraged from providing for their families and elderly parents when they knew that they could be thrown on the rates. They were convinced that the Poor Law was undermining the economy by interfering with "natural" laws:

"It appears to the pauper that the Government has undertaken to repeal, in his favour, the ordinary laws of nature; to enact that the children shall not suffer for the misconduct of their parents, the wife for that of her husband, or the husband for that of his wife: that no one shall lose the means of comfortable subsistence, whatever be his indolence, prodigality, or vice: in short, that the penalty which after all, must be paid by someone for idleness and improvidence, is to fall, not on the guilty person or his family, but on the proprietors of the lands and houses encumbered by his settlement. Can we wonder if the uneducated are seduced into approving a system which aims its allurements at the weakest parts of our nature – which offers marriage to the young, security to the anxious, ease to the lazy and impunity to the profligate".

The Commissioners suggested that the administration of the system, with its perceived inefficiencies and corruption, should be replaced by a more unified, efficient system, regulated by a locally appointed board, with direction from central government. The centre of the new system was to be the Workhouse, not the old local Poor House, the receptacle for the helpless, poor and aged, but a new, purpose-built institutional building which had the aim simultaneously to:

"relieve the helpless, deter the idle, set children on the right path, encourage thrift and temperance, reduce crime, improve agriculture, raise wages and heal the growing divisions in the social order".

Because it was thought that many parishes were too small to carry a workhouse of adequate size, several were grouped together to form a Workhouse Union, with one central facility administered by professional staff.

Outdoor relief was abolished altogether – although in certain parts of the country this was ignored – and all people claiming relief were forced to enter the workhouse where, as a deterrent, the living conditions were deliberately made much inferior to the conditions of the lowest paid worker outside. The "Workhouse Test" ensured that only the "deserving" cases were admitted and in truth only the really desperate availed themselves of the privilege.

The Poor Law Commission set up in 1834 upon the recommendation of the Royal Commission, had three commissioners and a secretariat headed by Edwin Chadwick, that champion of public health reform. Assistant Commissioners backed by an Inspectorate manned by civil servants, handled matters at local level, although their powers were of restraint and persuasion only; they could not force Guardians either to close an unsatisfactory poor house or build a new one. The maximum sum by way of improvement which they could insist should be spent on the buildings was £50 only, or one tenth of the average annual rate. Moreover, such powers as they had could only operate through the process of a writ of mandamus, a long and cumbersome process.

The Inspectorate, including the Assistant Commissioners, was a new feature of British administration; not the very first, since the Factory Inspectorate had preceded it by a year, but unlike that body, The Poor Law Inspectorate, as it was called, had a duty to be constructive as well as supervisory. Its members had to decide which parishes should be united and what should be the conditions surrounding the appointment of the Guardians. Each Assistant Commissioner had a salary of £700 per annum plus expenses. There were fifteen of them in 1835, although the number was reduced to nine in 1842, between them covering the rural counties. Most of them were the younger sons of the landed gentry which equipped them to speak to the landowners from whose tenants the boards of guardians were recruited.

The new workhouses, so like prisons that they were termed "bastilles", were architect designed on the so-called "panopticon" principle. This design generally was cruciform in shape with a central observation tower over the master's quarters. A rectangular boundary wall enclosed the whole building, interacting with the wards to give four courtyards rather like the cruciform hospitals of mediaeval times, each for a different class of pauper, male, female, young and old. Families were separated upon entering with even man and wife kept apart, and all their worldly possessions including their clothes were taken from them, to be replaced by the workhouse uniform. Alcohol and tobacco were banned and a vicious regime of hygiene imposed, not just to ensure good health but as a discipline in itself. The pauper could not leave the building without the express approval of the master, unless of course he wished to discharge himself, which would of course deprive him of relief.

Able-bodied paupers were set to work breaking stones, grinding corn, or picking oakum. The punishment regime was severe and in some cases inhuman. In the Warwick workhouse a two and a half year old child was punished for dirtying itself by forcing its excrement into its mouth; at the Hoo Union workhouse teenage girls were flogged by the master and at the notorious Andover workhouse, the paupers were so hungry that they fought amongst themselves for the gristle and marrow in the bones they were set to crush.

The old were not treated much better; Charles Dickens (1812-70) in 1860 described conditions in the Wapping workhouse as follows:

"None but those who have attentively observed such scenes, can conceive the extraordinary variety of expression still latent under the general monotony and uniformity of colour, attitude and condition. The form a little coiled up and turning away, as though it had turned its back on this world for ever; the uninterested face at once lead-coloured and yellow, looking passively upwards from the pillow; the haggard mouth a little dropped, the hand outside the coverlet, so dull and indifferent ... those were on every pallet; but when I stopped beside a bed, and said ever so slight a word to the figure lying there, the ghost of the old character came into the face."

Dickens' most famous character Oliver Twist epitomised in people's imagination the Victorian workhouse, although it is significant that the novel was published in 1837, only three years after the Poor Law Amendment Act of 1834, and so could only have described the old style poor house.

There was, nevertheless, a great deal of opposition to the new workhouses, not just from the poor themselves, but from the enlightened few in the more fortunate classes of society, who were becoming more and more concerned at the plight of the lower orders.

The scandal of the Andover workhouse which broke in 1845 brought down the Poor Law Commission and from 1847 until 1871 responsibility was passed to the Poor Law Board, although the Board never met. From 1871 until 1919 the Local Government Board had responsibility for Poor Law administration, and from 1919 until 1929 the Ministry of Health was the responsible department.

*   *   *   *   *   *   *

What the Poor Law Commission was to the workhouse, the Charity Commission was to almshouses. The Charity Commission was set up under the Charitable Trusts Act of 1855 following a series of scandals which rocked mid-Victorian society.

Until then corruption had been endemic in the management of charitable undertakings, particularly long established hospital and almshouse charities in whose master or warden the ownership of the assets was usually vested. As seen in previous chapters, many foundations dating from mediaeval times had large landholdings which, as time went by, produced huge incomes, far more than was really necessary for the maintenance of the inmates. The fictitious Hiram's Hospital in Anthony Trollope's novel *The Warden* deals with just such a situation where the kindly Rev. Septimus Harding, the hospital's warden, lives in a degree of comfort from the income derived from the foundation, oblivious that, strictly speaking, under the terms of the bequest, the income should have been spent on the eleven old men who comprised the brotherhood. The remorse experienced by the gentle old man and the subsequent gutter-press publicity leading to his resignation, form the opening scenes in the evergreen *Barsetshire Chronicles*.

The real life scandal which is thought to have given Trollope the plot for *The Warden* was centred on Winchester's Hospital of St. Cross, again referred to in an earlier chapter. The Rev. Francis North was the son of the Bishop of Winchester and a nephew of the then Prime Minister, Lord North when, in 1808 he was appointed by his father to the hospital's mastership. He did not live in, having a much more comfortable home in the Rectory of Old Alresford. The living there had also been given to him by his father, but he pocketed most of the income from the foundation over the forty years that he was master. When the story broke, the press had a field day and the affair was the subject of discussion in the House of Commons, following which the Attorney General instituted an Inquiry in the Court of Chancery. By this time the Rev. North, an old man of seventy-seven, had been created the Earl of Guildford. At first he defended himself vigorously and ultimately tried to resign, although the then bishop refused to accept his resignation until the Inquiry had reported. This it did in 1853, finding the earl guilty of misappropriation of the hospital funds. He was ordered to repay certain monies, but in the event only repaid about £4,000 compared with the estimated £300,000 which he had during his tenure. He resigned in 1855, the year that *The Warden* was published.

The Charity Commission was set up soon after to safeguard charities and particularly the income from their endowments. This was especially so in the case of educational charities where available money was not being used to best effect. For instance, they found that in the case of Dulwich College, a combined almshouse and school, the bedesmen were growing fat at the expense of the scholars. As a result of the Charity Commissioners' intervention, the educational establishment was hived off as a separate entity with its own endowment.

The basic law relating to charities dates from 1601; from the Charitable Uses Act of that year, and the definition of what constitutes a charity is found in the Act's preamble:

"Relief of aged impotent and poor people....the maintenance of sick and maimed soldiers and mariners, schools of learning ,free schools and scholars in universities....the repair of bridges, ports, havens, causeways, churches....and others".

This definition was refined in 1891 by Lord MacNaughten in what has since been known as the Pemsel Case, as follows:

"Charity in its legal sense comprises four principal divisions – trusts for the relief of poverty, trusts for the advancement of education, trusts for the advancement of religion, and trusts for other purposes beneficial to the community, not falling under any of the previous heads.".

The powers of the Charity Commission have evolved over the years since its inception with the current relevant legislation being the Charities Act 1991. Most of the older charities are governed by Trust Deed, but from its earliest days the principal instrument used by the Charity Commissioners for newly formed charities, and for control and supervision has been "the scheme".

A charitable scheme is nothing more than a formal statement of what is the charity's purpose, who are its trustees, what are their duties and responsibilities, what are its assets and in particular, what is its income.

The law of trusts is complex, but a fundamental premise affecting all trusts is the principle that no change may be made to the purpose or benefit derived for which the trust was originally set up. This is referred to as the doctrine of "cy-près", from the Norman French, meaning roughly "close to". Down the years since 1857 there have been attempts to relax the doctrine because, it was argued, it often gave rise to confusion among trustees and was seen as stifling new initiatives and inhibiting change, particularly in the case of parochial charities. The latest consideration of this matter followed the Woodfield Report on Charities published in 1988, but the view taken by the Charity Commissioners and endorsed by government was that the doctrine of "cy-près" was very flexible and that to bind it by actual legislation would inhibit its evolution and narrow its scope.

Day-to-day control of the 165,000 odd charities is administered through the "scheme" and whenever a charity having a Trust Deed approaches the Commissioners to effect some change or other, such as the mortgaging of property, the opportunity to replace it with a scheme is usually taken. This and the submission of an annual return and accounts is usually sufficient control, although since 1988 it has been the practice to amalgamate, under a new scheme, certain local charities with an income of less than £200.

There are now charities for all sorts of, some may think, strange purposes. But the importance of religion as a "fundamental spring of charity" must not be forgotten, and it was the resurgence of religious belief among many nouveaux riches Victorians which led to the building of so many groups of almshouses throughout the country, predominantly in the industrial north and in Greater London.

The Georgians were not very religious and the upper crust did not insist on their underlings attending church as their predecessors or successors, the Victorians, did. On Sunday 30th March 1851 the one and only census of religious attendance carried out in this country was undertaken, which showed that out of an available population, taking into account children, invalids, the aged and those having to work, of some twelve million people sixty percent or seven million people attended church or chapel. Attendance in rural areas and small towns was noticeably higher than in large towns; Church of England attendance predominated in the rural areas and the south; non-conformist attendance predominated in the newly expanding towns of the north.

It was not what we would today estimate to be the good attendance which attracted surprise at the time, but the forty percent that had stayed away! In particular, it was noticed that it was the working classes who were absent. The working classes tended to equate the Tory ruling classes with religious observance, and particularly with the Church of England, as it was then as now, very much part of the Establishment. And so, with the growing relative independence of industrial, rather than agricultural labour, many workers made their protest by staying in bed on Sundays.

From 1836 changes in attitude of some members of the Church of England was discernible. "Slum Parsons" emerged with sympathy for the Chartist reforms and an increased fervour for parochial work, particularly in industrial areas. There was an insistence in many quarters, born perhaps out of guilt, that the middle, lay and clerical classes had a duty to the labouring classes which resulted in the provision of clothing clubs, soup kitchens, parochial schools and almshouses.

In the industrial north, particularly the West Riding of Yorkshire, non-conformist dissent predominated. Mainly a layman's religion and by encouraging participation through preaching, Sunday School work and collective control through committees of elders, fitted many emerging young industrialists for a future career, whether it be in business or, after the Reform Acts, as members of Parliament. William Lovett, the Chartist leader encapsulated the mood of many of his contemporaries when he stated that "we must come to look upon practical Christianity as a union for the promotion of brotherly kindness and good deeds to one another".

Believer and unbeliever alike – and there were many unbelievers in the emerging ruling classes – shared then an ethical standard which was almost puritanical in its outlook, with a rectitude and devotion to duty as fervent as any which had preceded it. This code of ethics, since termed "evangelicalism", found its outlet in philanthropy and schemes of social reform calculated to mitigate the evils of the new industrial society without changing them. Out of this, the last great period of almshouse building emerged.

By and large, the vast majority of Victorian almshouses were provided in modest groupings of between five and twelve dwellings, generally single-storey with unexceptional architectural features. Most towns and many villages throughout the country had at least one such grouping; some more, with as in previous centuries, a predominance in Yorkshire and the London area.

Lady Hewley's Almshouses of 1840, situated off St. Saviourgate in York, is just such a group; twelve stone-built cottages with a tiny chapel built into the corner where the street changes direction. Only a plaque on the St. Saviourgate frontage betrays the presence of this unpretentious, unobtrusive home for retired ladies from York and the surrounding district. Slightly more flamboyant are the eight Tudoresque almshouses built twenty miles or so to the south in Wakefield, under the will of Dr. Caleb Crowther who died in 1840. Standing at the junction of George Street with Thornhill Street the predominantly single-storey cottages have a central two-storey feature housing a boardroom over one of the cottages. Each entrance doorway has a five-centred arch with dripstone over, as have the windows, with tall stone chimney-stacks and picturesque barge-boarding to the gable ends (Plate 55). The almshouses were to be occupied only by "Christian dissenters from the Church of England, of any denomination but Roman Catholics". This policy was extended to the twelve governors who were recruited from the largest dissenting churches situated within a mile of Wakefield's market cross. No Roman Catholic, attorney-at-law, or solicitor was ever to be elected as governor and those chosen had to affirm that they had never in the past been or would ever in the future be a member of the Church of England or "profess or act in support of those opinions or politics which are commonly called Tory or Conservative".

The growth of London, over the years, brought about the relocation of many almshouse groups, partly because of natural disasters such as the Great Fire, partly because their sites became more valuable, particularly those near to the centre, and partly because new land uses became necessary as a result of progress in housing and public health. St. Martin-in-the-Fields Almshouses were affected by such changes. They stood originally, before 1681, near Charing Cross, but in that year they were relocated in Charing Cross Road, housing sixty old ladies from the parish of St. Martin-in-the-Fields. By the close of the 18th century a need was established for a new burial ground on land occupied by the almshouses. As they were considered to be in need of replacement anyway, they were relocated again in 1818, this time in Camden Town, at the junction of Bayham Street and Pratt Street. Two-storey, of brick with stone dressings, the original chapel at the rear has in the interim been converted into dwellings (Plate 56). The Camden Town and Kentish Town Almshouses of about the same date, founded by Mrs Esther Greenwood of Regents Park, stand in Rousden Street off Camden Road. Tudoresque, of brick with cream render, they are typical of residential property in the heart of a densely packed metropolis (Plate 57). By contrast, the St. Pancras Almshouses of 1850 (Plate 58), situated not far away in Southampton Road are surrounded by a leafy garden where in summer the occupants can sit out to enjoy the flowers. Built of London brick with Picturesque porches and large airy windows, the almshouses provide generous accommodation not normally found in this part of the city. On the other side of the city, closer to the river, the United Westminster Almshouses in Rochester Row were built in 1881 to replace three old established groups, the Emery Hill Almshouses, built in 1708, the Rev. James Palmer's Almshouses of 1656 and Nicholas Butler's Almshouses of 1675. The United Westminster Group comprise thirty residences in a three-storey brick institutional building with Dutch gables and chimney stacks. The block also provides accommodation for a matron, a caretaker and a warden, and in doing so anticipated modern elderly person provision in sheltered housing schemes.

As might be expected, the cathedral city of Wells in Somerset has several groups of almshouses, although surprisingly most of them are Victorian in origin. We have referred in an earlier chapter to Bishop Bubwith's Almshouses of 1424 which incorporated the original Parish Guildhall. Around the parish church of St. Cuthbert, a hundred yards or so to the west of the cathedral, are situated three groups, Still's Almshouses, Llewellyn's Almshouses and Brick's Almshouses, all built at various times during the nineteenth century. Llewellyn's Almshouses in Priest's Row comprise two rows of brick-built dwellings facing each other across a narrow courtyard with an arched gateway at the Priest's Row end (Plate 59). Still's Almshouses are less imposing – stone-built, again round a close – and the much more visible Brick's Almshouses which face on to the churchyard which are also stone-built with Sedila-like porches .

Most of the nineteenth century almshouse groups described so far have little to commend them from the architectural standpoint but, as might be expected in this age of exuberance, there were many more throughout the country which demonstrated the best of the Victorians' sense of dignity and monumentality.

In the north-east, at Tynemouth, the Tyne Master Mariners' Asylum of 1836 displays a sense of dignity and repose which is the very epitome of the almshouse tradition. Constructed of tooled stone, with Dutch gables and an Italianate campanile, the asylum occupies an elevated position amongst landscaped grounds which set off the building to its best advantage. Recent renovation and improvement works have left the building unimpaired architecturally and fit for its purpose for a further one hundred and fifty years (Plate 60).

Moving further south, to the West Riding of Yorkshire, a spate of building during the middle and late years of the nineteenth century produced a whole series of architecturally important almshouses.

Sir Titus Salt, having made his fortune spinning the wool of the alpaca from South America, started to build what turned out to be the most famous model village in England in 1853 at Saltaire, a few miles to the north of Bradford. The village, complete with shops, churches and chapels, parks, a school, a hospital, a club, a library, a laboratory, a billiards room, an assembly hall, a gymnasium, an art school, a chess room and a lecture theatre, but no public houses, was laid out around an enormous spinning mill. It was as long as St. Paul's Cathedral with a chimney 250 feet high, modelled on the bell tower of St. Maria Gloriosa in Venice. The public buildings, built of stone, were also designed in the Italianate style, as were the 850 or so dwellings, of which 45 were almshouses. Erected around Alexandra Square, the almshouses were built to resemble miniature Italian villas, mainly single-storey, although two at each side opposite each other were two-storey. On the roof of the two-storey houses was placed a bell turret, whilst under each gable was carved the initials T.S. and C.S. in monogram, to commemorate Sir Titus and his wife, Caroline, supported by decorative acanthus leaf foliage carved in stone. All dwellings had a parlour with oven and boiler, bedroom and pantry. Preference was given to people who had worked in the mill and were known to Sir Titus or, after his death, to the trustees of the estate; but others of good character were eligible. Tenancy conditions were strict; the houses were actually inspected regularly to make sure that they were kept tidy and that the occupants were themselves clean and sober. Occupants lived rent free; married couples received a dole of ten shillings per week and single persons seven shillings and six pence. A chapel was provided for the pensioners in the north-west corner to save them having to walk far to worship, especially in winter. The building is, however, no longer used as a place of worship, having in recent years been converted into another dwelling. Adjacent to the almshouses, on the east side of the square, Salt provided a small hospital with three wards of nine beds each, one for men, one for women and one for children. It had its own dispensary and surgery where accidents could be dealt with urgently. The hospital was not solely for the almspeople, although it is likely that they made the most use of its facilities.

Across the city of Bradford, at Lilley Croft, in Heaton Road, to the west of the city centre, another important almshouse group was being erected at about the same time as Saltaire. The Bradford Tradesmen's Homes charity was set up in 1856, its purpose being to provide retirement accommodation for the tradesmen of Bradford and their dependants who had fallen on hard times and were no longer able to support themselves. The foundation stone was actually laid by Sir Titus Salt, who donated two thousand guineas, a magnificent sum at the time. With this and other donations, the first three blocks comprising thirty dwellings were completed at a cost of some £15,000. Later, in 1878, a fourth block of thirteen dwellings was erected by Mrs Elizabeth Wright in memory of her husband at a cost of some £5,200. The present estate comprises the forty-three almshouses, a master's or secretary's house and a chapel, all of which are listed Grade II under the Listed Buildings legislation. The rectilinear plan encloses an area containing lawns and flower beds with sitting out areas for the occupants slate roofs and tall chimneys have generous ground floor rooms, with two bedrooms built into the roof space with neat dormers. The chapel is situated in the centre of the northern block and can accommodate some three hundred people. Beautiful stained glass windows were subsequently donated in memory of local worthies, notably Sir Titus Salt, and a clock was donated in 1897 in memory of Mr James Drummond. The clock has since been converted to an electrical movement. All the dwellings, including the secretaries' house have recently been modernised with public sector grants. Bathrooms have been provided, together with up-to-date kitchen fittings and central heating (Plate 61).

Moving a little further south, to Halifax, two further monumental groups were provided by the brothers, Sir Francis and Joseph Crossley, whose carpet mill at Dean Clough was the largest in the world at the time. Sir Francis had in 1850 commissioned the building of a mansion, Belle View in Hopwood Lane, in the French Renaissance style, for his own occupation. In 1855, he built on adjoining land a group of almshouses in a similar style, ostensibly to house his aging work people, but in reality to act as an embellishment to his mansion. The two-storey, stone dwellinghouses front on to Margaret Street behind a low boundary wall with neat gardens (Plate 62).

Two hundred yards to the south, across Joseph Paxton's People's Park in Arden Road, his brother Joseph built, eight years later in 1863, another group set in landscaped gardens, this time around an open square facing due east. Of dark millstone grit under a Yorkshire slate roof, the design of the group was reminiscent of the Tudor period with Gothic window details and crenellated tower over the chapel (Plate 63).

Perhaps the most imposing Victorian almshouse in Yorkshire is situated at Aberford on the outskirts of Leeds, where the Gascoigne sisters, daughters of the local squire, erected a group as a monument to their father. The buildings, in white limestone, were commenced in 1844 and consisted of eight dwellings, four for men and four for women, separated by a lofty entrance hall with clock tower over, together with chapel at one end and dining – room at the other, the whole design in Victorian high gothick (Plate 64). The almsfolk were looked after by a matron who had her own cottage in the extensive grounds, and the whole charity was administered by trustees drawn from the local clergy. As with many almshouses built with motives other than strictly the provision of good housing, the Gascoigne Almshouses are no longer in use for their original purpose, the local authority museum service having taken them over as conservation workshops. New almshouses were provided during recent years with more up-to-date accommodation nearer to Aberford.

On Yorkshire's east coast, at Whitby in 1842 Sir George Gilbert Scott (1811-78) that most prolific of Victorian architects, designed the Seamen's Houses in Jacobean style (Plate 65), whilst Pugin, his contemporary, in 1847, designed St. Anne's Bedehouse at Lincoln for Richard Waldo Sibthorpe. Breaking away from mock Tudor, the almshouses were of single-storey in brick with stone dressings and had a chapel and warden's house (Plate 66). Sir George Gilbert Scott was active throughout the whole country, for example at Winchcome in Gloucestershire where in 1865 he built the Sudely Almshouses and, appropriately, at Godstone in Surrey he designed the St. Mary's Homes in asymmetrical half-timbered style.

Queen Victoria's Diamond Jubilee in 1897 spawned many almshouse groups, notably the Diamond Jubilee Cottage Trust, Wicken, Cambridge-shire, and Hartlepool's Diamond Jubilee Almshouses. The Queen herself (1819-1901) endowed a magnificent group at Whippingham on the Isle of Wight, to house the retired servants of Osborne. The almshouses were built on the opposite side of the road to Prince Albert's Parish Church, of red brick and tile with matching terracotta detailing on a stone plinth. The whole design is half Picturesque with lozenge-shaped window panes, tall chimney stacks and buttressed porches.

As might be imagined, London at the time the wealthiest capital in the world, produced some of the most magnificent almshouse groups. Four stand out particularly.

Following the success of the Licensed Victuallers' Benevolent Institution, founded in 1827 and to be described in detail in the next chapter, the Metropolitan Beer and Wine Trades Society built an asylum in 1852 on land adjoining Nunhead Green, in Southwark. Again a mock Tudor design was chosen, of brick with stone dressings, heavily buttressed with five centred arches to all entrances and tall chimneys built on the skew (Plate 67). The Free Watermen and Lightermen's Asylum in High Road, Penge, were built between 1840 and 1841. Of grey brick with again Tudoresque crenellated gatehouse, the almshouses occupy three sides of a landscaped quadrangle with trestled walkways across the garden and eccentric statues. Not far away in St. Johns Road, again in Penge, is situated the King William IV Naval Asylum, built by Queen Adelaide in 1847 as a memorial to King William, whose brief reign spanned the years 1830-1837. Much more truly Tudoresque than the previous group, the building has five centred arches to windows and door surrounds, tall octagonal chimney stacks and chequered brickwork to gable ends. Sadly, the building is no longer used as an almshouse, although it is used for council housing (Plate 68).

Finally, Sir William Powell's foundation adjoining Fulham's parish church, was endowed in 1680 and was rebuilt on its present site in 1869. L-shaped, around a leafy courtyard, the almshouses catch the full sunlight which throws into high relief the high Gothic details of the loggia and dormer windows. At the entrance, a heavily ornamented campanile houses figures of Faith, Hope and Charity in deep niches, with the inscription "God's Providence, Our Inheritance".

Plate 55. Dr. Caleb Crowther's Almshouses, Wakefield, West Yorkshire.

Plate 56. St Martin-in-the-Fields Almshouses, Camden, London.

Plate 57. Camden Town and Kentish Town Almshouses, Camden, London.

Plate 58. St. Pancras Almshouses, Southampton Row, London.

150

Plate 59. Llewellyn's Almshouses, Wells, Somerset.

Plate 60. *Tyne Master Mariners' Asylum, Tynemouth, Tyne and Wear.*

Plate 61. *Bradford Tradesmen's Homes, Lillycroft, Bradford, West Yorkshire.*

152

Plate 62. Sir Francis Crossley's Almshouses, Halifax, West Yorkshire.

Plate 63. Joseph Crossley's Almshouse, Halifax, West Yorkshire.

*Plate 64. Aberford
Almshouses, West
Yorkshire.*

*Plate 65. Seamen's
Houses, Whitby, North
Yorkshire.*

Plate 66. St. Anne's Bedehouses, Lincoln, Lincolnshire.

Plate 67. Metropolitan Beer and Wine Trade Asylum, Southwark, London.

Plate 68. King William IV Naval Asylum, Penge, London.

Chapter 11

The Present-day

With the coming of the twentieth century the provision of almshouses gradually diminished until now, near its end, hardly any new ones are being built. The reasons for this are many and various.

The principal reason has been a change in the status of working class people generally and old people in particular. From Edwardian times onwards, and especially since the First World War, the dependence of the workforce on the patronage of the landed gentry and the industrial employers has reduced. Home ownership is now over sixty percent. Government has assumed greater responsibility for social welfare and with increasing regular earnings and mobility, people are able to make their own provision for old age, either through personal pension arrangements or, at the very least, by qualifying for the state old-age pension.

The incidence of charitable giving has also changed markedly in recent years. In late Victorian times certain industrial philanthropists, generally Quakers, began social inquiry and experimentation which had far reaching effects on the housing conditions of the working classes. As we have seen, Engels and others documented the plight of the urban poor and in 1879 the Cadbury brothers, George and Richard, began to build a model village at Bournville on the outskirts of Birmingham which was to be an example for all public sector housing for over half a century. The Cadburys had in turn derived inspiration from the co-operative endeavours of Robert Owen at New Lanark and industrial reformers such as Sir Titus Salt , who as mentioned in the previous chapter, had built the first English model village of any consequence at Saltaire on the outskirts of Bradford in 1850. Benjamin Disraeli (1804-1881) contributed indirectly to the housing reform movement also; his best selling novel, *Sybil*, extolled the virtues of philanthropy through the provision of good housing to rent.

In 1904 Joseph Rowntree, a chocolate manufacturer living in York observed the damage to family life which was being brought about by bad housing conditions there. Overcrowding and lack of personal outdoor living space drove the breadwinner into the ale-house where his meagre earnings were dissipated to the detriment of his family. Rowntree reasoned that if working class families could be given decent houses with gardens where the menfolk could be usefully and profitably employed, family life might be enriched and, as a by-product, industrial output might be improved. Accordingly, he caused a model village to be built, New Earswick, near to his chocolate factory on the outskirts of York. The village was laid out with spacious rows of modern houses and gardens, interspersed with allotments and public open space. Shops and schools were provided, as well as special dwellings, bungalows, for those who had grown too old to work. These were not almshouses in the strict sense of the word since the Rowntree Trust was a registered charity in its own right, but they served the same purpose.

About this time too, in the London area, other philanthropists were making a slightly different but significant contribution to housing the poor.

Thomas Sutton, Edward Cecil Guinness and George Peabody set up charitable trusts whose objects were to provide housing to rent for the working classes. These of course tended to be tenement dwellings for families in the more densely populated areas of the metropolis, but again, the aged were not forgotten.

Housing Associations, as we now know them, also emerged at this time. The first, the Society for Improvement of the Conditions of the Labouring Classes was set up in 1830, to be quickly followed by a plethora of others, spreading to all the main cities in the country.

In 1888 the first municipal housing authority, the London County Council was formed, whose example was again copied nationwide. Responsibility for housing was passing from private philanthropic hands into the public domain. The main thrust of the new housing movement was still to provide family accommodation, but as heads of households grew older, special, generally smaller dwellings were also provided for their needs. Regularly, throughout the early years of this century, Acts of Parliament were passed which made provision both for improving existing housing and the building of new. At the peak in 1965 four hundred thousand homes a year were being built by local authorities with a generous proportion for elderly people.

The provision of medical care for the elderly also had its roots in the early years of the century. Florence Nightingale had inspired the infant nursing profession and again with the support from successive enlightened governments, local health care through general practitioners and cottage hospitals became available to all. This was carried to its zenith in 1948 when, following the Beverage report, the new Labour government set up a National Health Service with free treatment for all and a system of old-age pensions paid for out of earnings. In theory, never again need the poor and sick suffer for lack of money.

But another, equally significant social change also had an effect on charitable relief. During the early years of the century many new outlets for charitable giving emerged. Charities were set up for such diverse needs as sick animals, sick and abused children, the blind, the deaf, those suffering from all sorts of diseases and illnesses as well as a plethora of other good causes. And in the late fifties, charitable giving expanded overseas with the forming of Oxfam, Save the Children and other like-minded bodies, who saw the plight of the starving millions of the Third World as greater than at home. There are many charities still catering solely for the aged and infirm; Help the Aged, Age Concern, Sue Ryder, to mention but three. But the general pattern is that of a spreading of resources across the whole spectrum of society, with the elderly now receiving only a proportion of the available relief.

Until the turn of the twentieth century almshouses were very much parochial institutions providing accomodation in small groups, located specifically to satisfy local needs. However, with the urbanisation which followed the Industrial Revolution, there followed the setting up of what might be called corporate almshouses, that is charities providing housing for the elderly with institutional needs over wide areas.

Among the first such corporate almshouses was the Durham Aged Mineworkers' Homes Association, founded in the City of Durham in 1898, with the aim of providing retirement bungalows for mineworkers through-out the whole of the Durham coalfield. The brainchild of Joseph Hopper, himself a one time mineworker, the homes were seen by Hopper as a logical extension of the superannuation scheme which had been set up by the National Union of Mineworkers and which at the time paid four shillings a week to each retired mineworker. Out of this he had to provide for himself and his wife (if he had one) food, clothing, heating and shelter. But housing was in any case very hard to find and much sought after by working mineworkers and their families. Mine owners who provided groups of cottages near to their mines preferred to have workers as tenants rather than pensioners. At first Hopper's idea of the subvention of sixpence a week per mineworker to pay for the building of the homes was ridiculed by most with influence, but he persisted with his vision and in 1899, just one year after the association's formation, the first bungalows were completed in the village of Haswell. Joseph Hopper died in 1909, but before doing so had every reason to be proud of the achievement of the Homes Association; small groups of bungalows were springing up throughout the whole of County Durham and by 1925 it could count over a thousand.

The association is still going strong today with well over one thousand two hundred homes in management and has recently completed a programme of modernisation of all the bungalows originally provided by levies from miners (Plate 69). It has also built several new developments, both in the form of bungalows and sheltered dwellings with full warden care.

Joseph Hopper's example was followed on the opposite bank of the River Tyne when the Northumberland Mineworkers' Aged Homes Association was formed in 1900. It too has over five hundred bungalows in management whose tenants' rents are subsidised by subventions from working mineworkers' pay.

After the 1914-1918 war, the perceived need for housing veterans spawned many local war memorial homes, as well as another Corporate almshouse charity, the North-East Railway Cottage Homes and Benefit Fund. The Fund was founded in 1919 to provide accommodation for the elderly, infirm and injured railwaymen returning home from the war, as part of the "Homes fit for Heroes" movement. It all started with a bequest from a Mrs Ellen Granger of £10,000 in memory of her brother, Tempest Anderson. A further sum of £1,000 was contributed by the railwaymen themselves, together with a pledge of up to £20,000 during the first three years of the fund's existence by the North-East Railway Company.

As constituted in 1921, the fund had a dual purpose. Firstly, and it must be said, primarily, it was to pay sickness benefit to railwaymen and their dependents during their working lives. This was accomplished, as was usual, by a system of contributions deducted from the men's wages. The other purpose, but of no less importance to the contributors, was the provision of cottage homes for their retirement, and to this end over the years some four hundred and forty dwellings were provided throughout the north-east in thirty-seven different locations from Leeds to Berwick-on-Tweed (Plate 70). Originally, the men paid one penny per week each into the fund and currently pay 10p. The objects of the organisation have changed slightly over the years and although it has retained its charitable status, it has ceased to be an almshouse in the strict sense of the word and is no longer affiliated to the National Association.

The Cottage Homes movement which had its origins in Edwardian times as an extension of the Garden City movement, promoted many groups of almshouses, two large groups of which are of national importance.

The Linen and Woollen Drapers' Homes at Mill Hill in north-west London was founded in 1900 by James Marshall, a London store magnate – he owned Marshall and Snellgroves – and provided one and two-storey cottages, generally of brick, although some were half-timbered, very much the vogue at the time (Plate 71). The almshouses were provided within a garden setting with a central facility, clubhouse and offices, again in a mock Elizabethan style. Although not all that unusual in itself, the Mill Hill scheme provided the model for one of the largest almshouses complex built to date, that at Whiteley Village in Surrey.

Whiteley Village was built as a consequence of a legacy by and as a memorial to William Whiteley, the "Universal Provider" and owner of the well-known Bayswater store. In 1911 the trustees of the Whiteley estate bought two hundred and thirty acres of land in Surrey and initiated a design competition which was won by Frank Atkinson, the architect of the Mill Hill scheme.

A consulting architect, Walter Cave, was appointed by the trustees to prepare the competition documents and oversee the competition. He saw the traditional almshouse grouping as the very essence of the English village. The cottage form provided a counterpoint to the institutional setting of municipal housing which was prevalent in the early years of the century, and the single-storey form was obviously most appropriate for the elderly and infirm. His task was not to design the whole of the village but to prepare a brief within which other professionals could work and as a basis for the architectural competition.

The winner, Atkinson, who as well as designing the Mill Hill scheme had also built the Selfridges store, responded by laying out a central circular area which was left in its natural, semi-wild state with rhododendrons and wild flowers. This was surrounded, firstly by a road flanked mainly by single-storey housing and, further out from the centre by an octagonal road with access roads radiating from it (Figure 44 and Plate 72). Housing for three hundred and fifty pensioners was provided, each cottage consisting of a living room with sleeping lobby, the traditional almshouse accommodation. A statue depicting the virtues of industry and enterprise was placed at the centre of the village.

The village was completed by the addition of village hall, store, library, church, both non-conformist and Roman Catholic chapels, public hall and club and restaurant. Since its inception, a special home for the frail elderly has been added, Whiteley House, housing thirty-eight single residents and five couples, together with a cottage hospital with thirty-five beds, which provides acute medical, post-surgical and permanent nursing care. The village runs its own bus service every weekday, ferrying residents to and from Walton-on-Thames. Each cottage has now been modernised and the estate is administered by the trustees, who keep the grounds immaculate, and each tenant is expected to cultivate his or her garden. All the almsfolk emanate from either commercial or agricultural occupations.

Similar developments were provided by the Douglas Haigh Memorial Homes, now Haigh Homes and the Royal British Legion village near Maidstone, not almshouses in the strict sense but further examples of purpose-built housing for the elderly.

The Licensed Victuallers' National Homes is another almshouse which became a national body during the mid-twentieth century. It was originally founded in 1826 as the Licensed Victuallers' Asylum by members of the licensed trade to provide for the needs, both housing and financial, of its members. Its actual stated aims were:

"to receive and maintain the decayed aged licensed victuallers and their wives or widows, and for the purpose, as far as it is in their power, of mitigating the evils of poverty and the ills consequent of old age".

The main need of course was for landlords and tenants of licensed premises who, after a lifetime of service to the brewery companies, had to find alternative accommodation when they retired.

Its first dwellings were provided at Peckham in London, but its magnus opus, at the time the largest concentration of old persons' housing in the country, was a development in the parish of St. Giles, Camberwell, off the Old Kent Road. Originally it was intended to build only forty-three dwellings on the site, which were erected around three sides of a grassy courtyard with an impressive classical central portico housing the chapel,

Fig 44. Plan of Whiteley Village, Surrey.

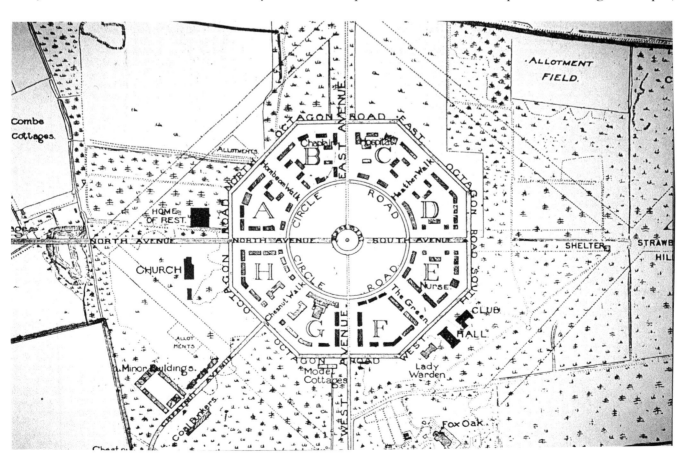

and surmounted by a squat tower. Further almshouses were added in three more wings surrounding the original buildings, giving a total of one hundred and seventy-six residences. A large ornamental gateway was added in 1927 to celebrate the centenary of almshouses.

Queen Victoria granted the Asylum a Royal Charter in 1842 and in 1884, again by Royal Charter, the objects of the charity were extended to allow payments to out-pensioners i.e. those eligible ex-licensees who were not lucky enough to have the tenancy of a dwelling owned by the Asylum. The name was changed firstly in 1919 to the Licensed Victuallers' Benevolent Institution, and finally in 1959 to the Licensed Victuallers' National Homes.

Apart from the Camberwell development, growth was very slow during the nineteenth and early twentieth centuries. But in 1959 a decision was taken to purchase a fifty-seven acre estate at Denham in Buckinghamshire and to build a garden village exclusively for retired members. Like Whiteley Village it has expanded into a self-contained centre, not only providing living accommodation, but also shops, a clubhouse and community centre and a nursing home, together with all the administrative offices of the society. The site in Camberwell was vacated although the original almshouses are now used as council housing. There are now some two hundred and fifty residents at Denham living in one hundred and ninety bungalows in near idyllic surroundings.

Not content with that achievement, in 1966 the trustees, at the suggestion of their patron, H.R.H. Prince Philip, decided to expand nationwide and have since built no less than sixteen estates modelled on Denham throughout the country from Brighton in the south to Newcastle in the north-east. These Edinburgh Estates as they are called, provide a further two hundred and seventy bungalows and flats, bringing the total provision up to almost six hundred and fifty homes.

A remarkable modern day example of philanthropy can be found at South Chailey, Haywards Heath, East Sussex. The Grantham Trust had been established in Chailey since 1951, founded under the will of Mrs Sybil Grantham to provide homes for elderly gentlewomen in distressed circumstances. In 1965 the local GP, Dr. Jack Palmer, formed an old folks' welfare committee with the aim of co-ordinating activities for the elderly people of the village. Following a survey of all the elderly residents, it became clear that the greatest anxiety that they had was that as they became frail and infirm they would no longer be able to cope with their current accommodation and may have to move away. What was needed was sheltered housing i.e. easily managed small flats or bungalows where they could live out their days independently yet under the watchful eye of a warden.

A housing association was formed with the object of building such sheltered accommodation and during its search for a suitable site, the committee made contact with the Grantham Trust who owned, among other assets, a field called Hoggs Mead in the south-east corner of the village.

During negotiations for the purchase of the land, it was clear that the two organisations had similar objects and with the agreement of the Charity Commision, the association took over the management of the trust, changing the wording of the trust deed from "distressed gentlewomen" to "poor women over 50".

Thirty-four flats were planned at Hoggs Mead, originally in five blocks. When the first block was completed in 1979, and named Palmer Court in memory of Dr. Jack Palmer, the trust ran out of money and, being a private trust, was not eligible for building grants or loans. However, three individuals eventually came forward with offers to provide finance to complete the development.

Mrs Christine Reckitt of Chailey Moat offered to fund the second block of six flats provided that they would house poor men as well as women. This was agreed to by the Charity Commissioners. The block was named Reed House, the middle name of her late husband.

Mrs Jean Follett Holt was then introduced to the trust by David Scott of The Almshouse Association who was aware that she wished to provide some almshouses in memory of her late husband, Colonel Frank Follett Holt. Having visited the site and seen the first two blocks, Mrs Follett Holt readily agreed to provide finance for the third block of seven flats, which when completed in 1984 were named Follett Holt House. Following an appeal through the local parish magazine, an anonymous donor funded the fourth block containing a further six flats, which was named Meadow Court. The whole development was constructed in the local "oasthouse" style of architecture and is one of the more striking almshouse developments built in recent years (Plate 73).

*   *   *   *   *   *

In February 1946 in the Chapter House of Southwark Cathedral a meeting was held of representatives of London's almshouses with a view to forming a committee to safeguard the interests of almshouse buildings and the welfare of almsfolk. Its actual terms of reference were:

"to safeguard the interests of almshouses and to promote the welfare of beneficiaries in view of the proposed changes of legislation."

Concern was expressed that these changes in legislation, which culminated in the National Assistance Act 1948, heralding the Welfare State, would adversely affect charitable institutions generally and almshouses in particular, since it was feared that statutory provision would supplant voluntary effort. After six long years of war many of London's one hundred and thirty-eight historic almshouses were in a poor state of repair. Many were empty and suffering from bomb damage. The London Almshouse Committee, as it was called, felt that almshouses were:

"of great potential benefit to aged people in keeping the spirit of voluntary service alive, whatever may be the bounty or pension assured by the State."

Pending details of the new legislation, a review of London's almshouses was undertaken and later a constitution was adopted. The Committee was renamed the Association of London Almshouses, and with a grant of £1,000 from the National Corporation for the Care of Old People a full-time member of staff was appointed, firstly as an appeals organiser and then as General Secretary. His name was Leonard Hackett. Supported by Miss R. G. M. McAuliffe the Hon. Secretary of the Association and incidentally, the convenor of the original meeting at Southwark, Hackett began a vigorous campaign to modernise substandard almshouses and, despite an acute problem with funding, made progress sufficient to encourage the committee to extend its remit to the whole country. In 1950 the Association became The National Association of Almshouses with the following aims:

To advise members on any matters concerning almshouses and the welfare of the elderly.

To promote improvements in almshouses.

To promote study and research into all matters affecting almshouses.

To keep under review existing and proposed legislation affecting almshouses and where necessary take action.

To make grants and loans to members.

To encourage the provision of almshouses.

With the increasingly complex legislation surrounding the improvement and day-to-day running of almshouses, trustees down the years have had reason to be grateful for the advice provided by the National Association, recently renamed The Almshouse Association. Now, headed by its current Director, David Scott, it represents the interests of over one thousand seven hundred and thirty charities owning some twenty-six thousand dwellings throughout the whole country.

The Executive Committee of The Almshouse Association is comprised of either trustees or clerks to trustees of member charities, with not more than one from each administrative county or district up to a total of twenty-five persons with the power to co-opt up to a maximum of five additional persons.

The present chairman since 1987, Lady Benson OBE, was elected to represent Wiltshire in 1978.

Mr Richard Brayne MBE, who has served on the Executive Committee since 1972 and as chairman from1981 to 1987, is the current master of the Ironmongers' Company which itself provided a founder-member of the original London Almshouse Committee.

It is the calibre and length of service of experienced regional members of the Executive Committee which help to provide such excellent support to almshouse charities throughout the country.

The Housing Association movement, of which almshouses are a part, was officially recognised and given encouragement by Government by the passing of the Housing Act 1974. Under this enactment the Housing Corporation, which had been set up ten years earlier to promote cost-rent and co-ownership housing, was given the responsibility of registering, regulating and funding all housing associations and of administering a special grant created for their needs, Housing Association Grant. This grant, providing in some cases one hundred percent finance, was available not only for the provision of new housing, but also for the rehabilitation, refurbishment and repair of existing stock. Almshouses formed a special branch of the Housing Association register, and the National Association lost no time in advising its members of the benefits of registration. During the late seventies and early eighties much of the almshouses stock that was capable of repair and improvement was brought up to modern standards and some that was not, was replaced with new. Naturally all buildings deteriorate with age and some become obsolete. Those that were not capable of sufficient improvement to provide acceptable residential accommodation by modern standards have, thankfully, found new uses, some as museums and others as commercial premises. Some, as in the case of Beamsley Hospital near Skipton, have been converted for use as holiday accommodation where several small almshouse dwellings have been combined to form one large unit. It is true to say that not all almshouses that are capable of improvement have yet been modernised, but a healthy ongoing programme is still in train.

* * * * * * *

In June 1986 a service of thanksgiving was held at Westminster Abbey in the presence of H.M. Queen Elizabeth the Queen Mother to celebrate one thousand years of almshouse provision in England. With that it would seem that our story has come full circle, since it marked the anniversary of the founding in 986 of St. Leonard's Hospital in York, mentioned in the opening chapter.

With the establishment of the welfare state and the plethora of agencies, both voluntary and commercial, as well as Local Authorities now caring for the aged in both purpose-built establishments and increasingly in their own homes, it may be imagined that the need for the type of care which almshouses trusts provide has diminished. Nothing could be further from the truth. With the increasing longevity now enjoyed by all sectors of society there remains a growing and sustained need for all types of aged persons' accommodation. It is likely that the almshouse movement will be still going strong in another thousand years. Let us hope so.

Plate 69. Durham Aged Mineworkers' Homes, County Durham.

Plate 70. North-East Railway Cottage Homes, Darlington, County Durham.

168

Plate 71. Linen and Woollen Draper's Homes, Mill Hill, London.

Plate 72. Whiteley Village, Surrey.

Plate 73. Follett House, Grantham Trust, South Chailey, Sussex.

Bibliography

Books

Bailey, Brian. *Almshouses*, Robert Hale, 1988.

Bean, David. *Tyneside, a Biography*, Macmillan, 1971.

Berridge, Clive. *The Almshouses of London*, Ashford, 1987.

Best, G. *Mid-Victorian Britain*, Fontana, 1971.

Briggs, Asa. *Victorian People*, Penguin, 1954.

Briggs, Asa. *Victorian Cities*, Penguin, 1963.

Burn W.L. *The Age of Equipoise*, Allen and Unwin, 1964.

Clay, Rotha Mary. *The Mediaeval Hospitals of England*, Frank Cass and Co., 1909.

Costello et al. *An Introduction to the Royal Hospital*, Kilmainham, 1987.

Darley, Gillian. *Villages of Vision*, Architectural Press, 1975.

Davis, Terence. *The Architecture of John Nash*, Studio Press, 1960.

Dickens, A.G. *The English Reformation*, Fontana, 1967.

Dolman, F.T. *Ancient Domestic Architecture*, 1858.

Doubleday, H.A. *Victoria County History of Yorkshire*, Inst. of Historical Research, 1907.

Elton, G.R. *England under the Tudors*, Methuen, 1958.

Godfrey, W. H. *The English Almshouse*, Faber and Faber,1950.

Hanson, Michael. *2,000 years of London*, Country Life, 1967.

Harrison, J.F.C. *Early Victorian Britain*, Fontana, 1979.

Harrison, J.F.C. *Late Victorian Britain*, Fontana, 1990.

Heath, Sidney. *Old English Houses of Alms*, Griffiths, 1910.

Helm, P.J. *Exploring Tudor England*, Robert Hale, 1981.

Jones, E. and Woodward, C. *A Guide to the Architecture of London*, Weidenfeld and Nicholson, 1983.

Kubler,George. *Building the Escorial*, Princeton Univ. Press, 1982.

Marshall, Dorothy. *English People in the 18th Century*, Greenwood Press, 1956.

Ordnance Survey. *Monastic Britain*, Ordnance Survey, 1976.

Pallister, D.M. *The Age of Elizabeth*, Longmans, 1983.

Parker, Roy. *English Society in the 18th Century*, Allen Lane, 1982.

Pevsner, Nicholas. *The Buildings of England*, Penguin, 1952.

Raphael, Mary. *The Romance of English Almshouses*, Mills and Boon, 1926.

Royal Commission on Hist. Monuments York, *Historic Buildings in the Central Area*, H.M.S.O, 1981.

Scarisbrick, J.J. *The Reformation and the English People*, Blackwell, 1984.

Schofield, John. *The Buildings of London from the Conquest to the Great Fire*, British Museum Publications, 1984.

Taylor, Kate. *Wakefield District Heritage*, Wakefield EAHY Committee.

Temple, Nigel. *John Nash and the Village Picturesque*, Alan Sutton, 1979.

Thompson, David. *England in the 19th Century*, Pelican, 1978.

Wearmouth, R.F. *The Working Class Movements of the Nineteenth Century*, Epworth Press, 1963.

Willis, M. *Nineteenth Century Britain*, Blackwell, 1990.

Wrighton, K. *English Society, 1580 - 1680*, Hutchinson, 1982.

Pamphlets

Mini guide to Worcester.

Hospital of William Brown, Stamford, Lincolnshire.

Lord Leycester's Hospital, Warwick.

Forde's Hospital, Coventry.

St. John's Hospital, Canterbury.

City of Wells Guide.

The Royal Hospital, Chelsea.

The Royal Hospital, Kilmainham, Dublin.

The Hospital of St. Cross.

The Holy Jesus Hospital and Joicey Museum, Newcastle-upon-Tyne.

The Commandery, Worcester.

City of Salisbury Guide.

Maritime Greenwich.

City of Winchester.

Evesham Abbey.

The Vale of Evesham.

Index